What is Your Dream?

Make your dream come true. Start today.

By the same author:

What is Your Excuse?

Have you found your Mr. Wong yet?

Readers' comments

'I got a huge urge to make my dreams come true. Right now!' **Isa**

'Don't be afraid to ask. That is what I learned.' **Sabrina**

'Not only is this book inspiring; it gave me the courage to continue dreaming, no matter what...' **Kirsten**

'I read the book in one sitting. I admire Esther and the others for the way they live their dreams. Now it's my turn.' **Cateleine**

'While reading, I couldn't help but dream about all the things I still want to experience...' **Ineke**

'I became an entrepreneur and started my own company! This book contributed to this achievement.' **Marco**

Visit www.estherjacobs.info for more information on her books, keynotes and workshops.

Esther Jacobs

What is Your Dream?

Make your dream come true. Start today.

NO! EXCUSES

Cover Image
Eef Ouwehand, www.eefphotography.com
Cover Design and original layout
Marieke Rinzema, Fuig text and design, NL
Layout adaptations for English version
Velin@Perseus-Design.com
Translation Dutch – English
Isa Mc Kechnie, Utrecht, The Netherlands

Originally published in Dutch in 2010
by A.W. Bruna Uitgevers B.V., Utrecht, NL.
'Wat is jouw droom?'
Reprint by author in 2013; www.estherjacobs.info
ISBN 978-90-6523-702-6

The memories you want for tomorrow
must be made today

Esther :)

Contents

Interviews

Martijn (37) set up an outdoor business, lost a lot of money in bankruptcy, and built a megalithic tomb with fourteen thousand people. Now he uses his organizational talents to bring together people, ideas and information in order to solve small and large problems.

'Auntie Leen' (88) was the only one in her family who survived the Second World War and concentration camp Auschwitz. In spite of this, she always believed in mankind's goodness. Now she dedicates herself to countering discrimination in schools.

Eef (36) used to dream of a career within the family business. When it went bankrupt she made a definite choice for her second passion: photography. A few times she chose to leave everything behind and completely start afresh, for example on Curaçao. Her motto is: 'Just do it!'

Anne-Lyne (56) is a teacher at an elementary school in Switzerland. Despite a serious illness, she worked in Madagascar for six months as a volunteer and fell in love with the country. Now she puts all her spare time and meager finances in small projects that she manages herself.

Maanwilla (38) is a speech therapist, a single mother of two, who is clairaudient. When she first discovered that she could hear more than others, she simply preferred to be 'normal'. After her divorce she decided to go for her passion, in which she can use all her talents. With ups and downs she started her own speech therapy practice. She also gives voice and presentation trainings to business people, politicians and academics.

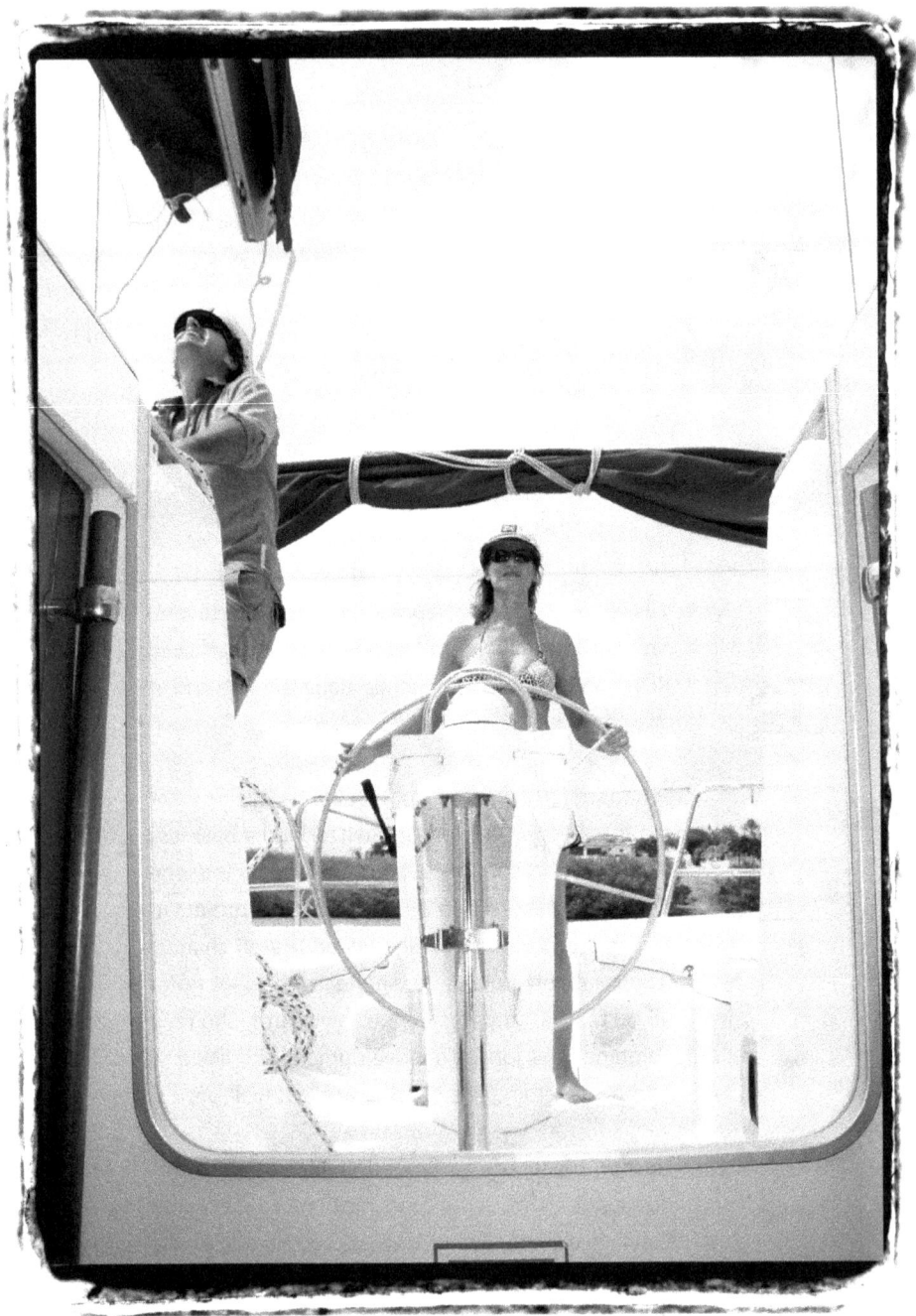

What is Your Dream?

I wrote this book on a yacht in the Caribbean. When my love and I sailed from island to island, I turned my own experiences and the stories of other dreamseekers into concrete tips:

- How do you find out what you really want?
- How can you make that important first step that many find so difficult?
- How to use networking and creativity?
- Which important choices will you have to make?

And last but not least:

- How can you persevere despite the obstacles you will undoubtedly run into?

As a teenager I already dreamed of sailing the Caribbean. However, I knew this was not realistic. I couldn't sail and didn't even know anybody who could sail. Let alone someone who had a boat and time to go with me. I decided to pursue other dreams.

Twenty years later I met my current boyfriend in Curaçao: a fervent sailor, with a boat, and geared up for adventure! It looked as though my dream would come true, after all. He taught me to sail in a little boat and... I found out I get seasick a lot.

However, we did end up going. We decided to compromise. He would sail his boat in four rough days and nights from Curaçao to the British Virgin Islands (BVI). I would fly over like a true luxury passenger, so we could make daytrips sailing from island to island.

Unfortunately, when we finally managed to make time for the trip, he had to turn back after one day because the engine of the boat broke down, which made it irresponsible to sail on.

Almost a year later we tried again, and with a different boat, the crossing went well. For two months we explored the beautiful islands of the Caribbean together. It is fantastic to visit so many different places, some of which are only reachable with your own boat. Each island has its own nature, culture and secrets.

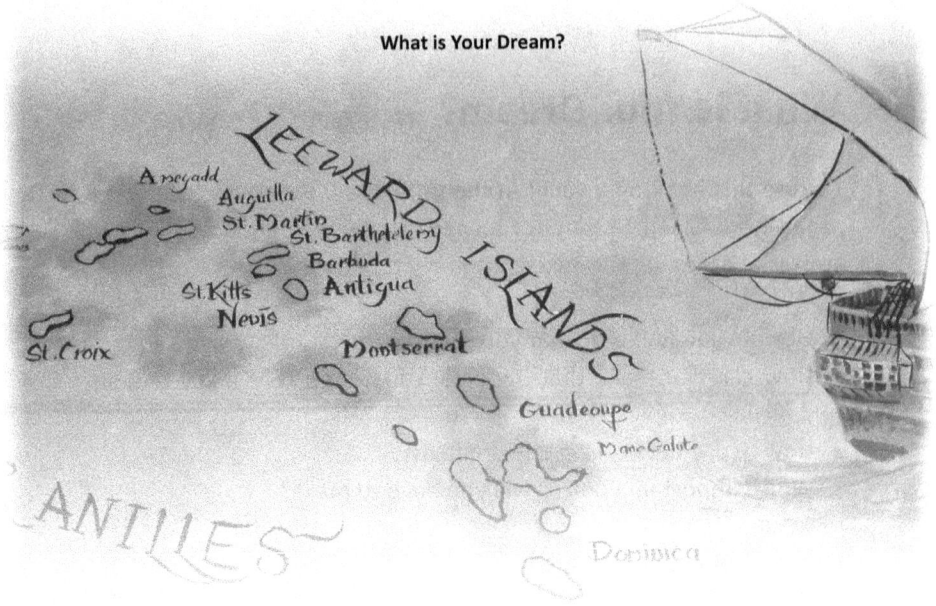

Illustration: map of Leeward Islands

And I must say that after a few days of feeling 'slightly wobbly', I was hardly ever seasick.

Perhaps the journey was even more fun exactly because I had spent all those years thinking it would never happen.

Following your dreams isn't always easy. There can be setbacks and things can turn out differently than expected. But the feeling of doing something that you always wanted to do is priceless, as is the energy this gives you.

During my travels through more than one hundred countries, with different cultures and living conditions, I met many exceptional people. A simple fisherman on Madagascar, the poorest and the wealthiest family of Guatemala, expats in the Caribbean, monks in Laos, westerners spreading their wings.

I learned that everyone has dreams. Big or small, nearby or seemingly unreachable, personal or for a 'greater good'. However different we may seem, all people have an important thing in common:

our eyes start to shine when we talk about the things that our hearts long for.

My grandmother was married to a grocer. Naturally, she worked in the shop her entire life. One day I asked her what she had always dreamed of becoming when she was a child. Briefly, she was lost in thought. Then that special look appeared in her eyes, a look I have come to recognize all over the world. 'I would have wanted to be a seamstress,' she said resolutely. 'Making beautiful things on one of those electrical machines, I would have liked that.'

The family of my Jewish grandfather died in the Holocaust. Granddad was a advertising illustrator and during his time in hiding he made the most beautiful drawings. However afterwards, as one

Illustration: drawing of my grandmother

of the few survivors of the war, he had to take over his family's clothing factory. His eyes only started to shine when he showed me his drawings, or, for example, a logo he had designed for my father's birthday.

My grandparents did not get the chance to pursue their dreams, like so many of our ancestors and people in developing countries. Some resign to this fact. Others create chances for themselves, regardless of their circumstances. Thankfully, more and more people of different ages and backgrounds belong to this second category.

What's the difference between having a dream and making it come true?

When it comes down to it, everyone knows what needs to be done in order to realize their dream. If you want to travel around the world, you have to quit your job, rent out your house, buy a ticket, pack your bags and...go! It is also clear what you have to do if you want to lose weight: eat less, stop snacking and get moving. Setting up your own business, too, or making more time for fun things, can be divided into easy steps. Most people know, more or less, what actions ought to be completed to make these dreams real, or where they can find information if they don't know it themselves. In short: the *mechanics* are clear. And yet, few people make the first step. Why? And how can you surpass this (apparent) barrier?

The secret is motivation. If you are really convinced of something, if you can think about nothing else and truly want it, then the fire in you has started to burn. Then you will find a way to reach what you want, even if the mechanics aren't all that clear. In this book you will find a number of mechanics-tips (including a few very clichéd ones), and above all a lot of inspiration to show you that it is truly possible to realize your dreams; whatever it is that you want.

I will take you on a journey along the shiny eyes of some people in our world. The stories are true, told by ordinary people like you and me. They wanted to make a trip through space, work for charity, build a megalithic tomb, have more leisure time, start their own business, become a surrogate mother, travel or emigrate. Some managed to reach their goals; others are still in the process or had to readjust their expectations. How did they take the difficult first step? How did they deal with setbacks and disappointments? What do their lives look like now?

Are you surprised by their dreams or do they seem familiar? Their stories might open your eyes and give you a better idea of your dream. Share their ups and downs, their frustrations and their euphoria. Let yourself be inspired by their triumphs and learn from their mistakes. Hopefully these stories will put your obstacles into perspective and you will dare to take a step into the direction of your dream.

In my first book, *What is Your Excuse?* I told my personal story about Coins for Care (how I raised $25 million for charity without any experience, a budget or a network), how I participated in Survivor, and how I set up numerous business ventures. Back then I consciously chose not to turn it into a how-to book. Many readers let me know that they appreciated this and that my experiences had inspired them. However, during the workshops 'realize your dream', which I started to give back then, I noticed that many people are actually in need of guidelines and concrete tips. Hence I mix both concepts in this book.

In *What is Your Dream?* you'll find seventeen refreshing, open-hearted interviews with people who are following their dreams. The most important tips given by them are combined with my own experiences and listed as 23 concrete tips. Maybe you only want to read the interviews; another moment you may want to get some advice or want to get started on the exercises. There is no fixed order to this book; it is up to you to determine what is applicable and appeals to you.

My most important advice is: do **something** today to get a step closer to your dream!

I wish you an inspiring journey.

Esther Jacobs
Juni 2010

© www.eefphotography.com

The first step to a destination

is deciding that you

refuse to remain

where you are right now.

The first step

You have a restless feeling, a vague wish or a cherished dream. The fact that you have become aware of this is the first step. Now you'll decide if you want to do something with it, or continue what you were doing before.

Think about the consequences of your decision. Is there a chance you'll regret it later?

Is it selfish to follow your dreams? I believe it is sometimes more important to follow your heart than to settle for what others expect from you.

You don't have to know exactly what you want. It is important to get moving. Now. Don't wait for the perfect moment; it will never come.

Don't get fixated on a certain idea. Look beyond your goals. If you find the first step difficult, make a hypothetical plan to help you cross that threshold. Don't burn your bridges behind you; take small steps towards your goal.

It doesn't matter if the outside world thinks your dream is not realistic. There are enough examples of people who realized 'impossible' dreams.

This part consists of the following chapters and interviews:

You're worth it!
You don't need to know what you want (but it helps!)
Interview with Daniëlle
Be realistic, or maybe not?
Interview with Rainer
Make a plan!
Interview with Hilda and Bas
Look beyond your goal
Interview with Sylvia
Don't wait for the right moment
Interview with Marnix
Take small steps
Interview with Adriaan

You're worth it!

Is it selfish to follow your dream? Many people tend to answer 'yes'. Many of us have been raised with the idea that you must first take care of others and only then think of yourself. Especially women may find this familiar. In my experience, however, it is easier to take care of others after you take care of yourself first.

Do you recognize that depressing, restless feeling when you are constantly caring for others and can't recharge your battery? You feel like you keep being overtaken by events and fail to do everything the way you intended to. You are easily agitated. What is left to give when the source is dry? What kind of example are you to your children if you can't set boundaries? It is important to take time for yourself and give attention to what you find important. Allow yourself this. Don't feel guilty if you think of yourself. On the contrary!

In an airplane they always show a safety procedure before take-off. They explain, among other things, that if cabin pressure drops, oxygen masks will appear. What do the flight attendants emphasize, here? That you should first put on your own oxygen mask and only then help others wear theirs, even when you are traveling with small children. In this case it is very clear and logical. Of course: if you can't breathe yourself, how can you help others breathe?

Why don't we apply this principle in ordinary life more often? Personally, I've always been a lone wolf who didn't care about main-

stream values. I notice that my mentality sometimes awakens strong feelings and reactions in others. Is it because they are not used to people doing as they please? Because they don't know how to react? Maybe they are jealous of my freedom? Or do they believe I am selfish if I put myself first in certain situations? I have noticed that the oxygen mask example sets people thinking. And that it often helps, especially women, to justify their choices. Feel free to use the oxygen mask metaphor where you see fit, and study the effect it has on yourself and others.

Sometimes it is difficult to break through existing patterns. Writer Paulo Coelho described this very eloquently with a bizarre example: the distance between the two tracks of most railroads in the world is exactly 143.5 cm, or 4 feet and 8.5 inches. Why this number? he asked himself. 'That's just the way things are,' he was told. Paulo went to find out and learned that modern railroads use this distance because it was the width of the old roads. And why was this? Because the Romans had calculated how wide two horses next to each other were, in those times: 143.5 cm. That's how the distance between the tracks of railroads, now used by ultramodern high-speed trains, was determined by the Romans!

When immigrants came to America and built new railroads, they kept the old standards. Just because they were used to them.

Exactly how limiting old patterns can be was experienced by the engineers who built the space shuttle. They wanted to build wider fuel tanks, but this was impossible because they had to be transported by rail, and the tunnels had not been designed for larger sizes. In this way, the Romans even influenced space travel...

Actually, there is no reason to continue using this distance, determined by the Romans, and yet it is used and accepted by everyone.

At some point in our own lives there is always that person who insists that things have to be done in a certain way. What if doing it differently is much more convenient? Courage is needed to break through existing patterns. The fact that you picked up this book means you are playing with the notion of tackling something in your life. Maybe this will help you to challenge the status quo. Keep asking questions and focus on your goals, not on the way things have always been...

You're worth it!
Right?

You don't need to know what you want (but it helps!)

Some people know exactly what they want; others don't have a clue. You don't need to have a concrete goal in mind; you might have a vague feeling of wanting something different. Or maybe there is something that makes you incredibly happy, but you have no idea what to do with it.

You don't have to know exactly where you want to go. Sometimes you only know that you want to leave. That you are no longer doing the right things. Do you recognize the feeling when everything feels heavy, 'sticky' almost and takes a lot of effort, but doesn't yield much energy? This can be a sign that you need to try something else. If you take the first step, the next step will become clear. And along the way it'll become easier and the flow will come naturally.

I, too, stopped with something that didn't make me happy, without knowing what it was that I did want. For seven years I worked as an unpaid volunteer for Dutch charity, and after Coins for Care and the Donor Organization I was fed up with charities and with the Netherlands. With a lot of effort I closed that chapter of my life and moved to Curaçao. I gave myself the freedom to do absolutely nothing for the first while. Also when someone approached me with a new fun project, or when I had an idea myself, I did not immediately act on it. I chose to get into something new only if it really enthused me and stuck with me for weeks. Sometimes I would lie in the hammock all day, without even reading a book; simply being in the moment. I didn't have to do anything, I didn't want to do anything, and I learned to accept this. A few months later I was browsing through some old files on my computer. I came across the concept of a book that I had once written and I enjoyed reading it so much that I chose to adjust it and finish it. I had found my new passion! The book *What is Your Excuse?* was published, and then this book followed, and then "Did you find Mr. Wrong yet?", and so on. Without knowing what I wanted in advance, a temporary void helped me find my new passion, and I became a writer!

© www.eefphotography.com

A bit further on you'll find an interview with Daniëlle (page 26). The only thing she knew for sure was that she wanted to leave the Netherlands. Based on this knowledge she took a few steps, without knowing where they might lead. She ended up in a place where she is happier. If she had stayed in the Netherlands until she knew exactly what she wanted, this would have probably never happened.

Rainer Nölvak was annoyed by the garbage that he found in the forests he loved so much, dreamt of a clean Estonia. He had no idea if it was possible to clean up his country and how he would undertake such a project. But because his vision of beautiful, clean forests set his heart alight, he decided to give it a try. On page 36 you'll read about his plan and the results.

EXERCISE FIND OUT WHAT YOU WANT

The following questions can help you get a clearer picture of your dream.

What would you do if you had only one day left to live?

What makes you completely happy and lose all track of time?

What did you enjoy doing as a child that you no longer do?

What would you do if you won the lottery?

What would you do if you had enough time and money, if you had no obligations and if you were sure that you couldn't fail?

If you can't immediately think of an idea, the following questions may help:

What place would you like to visit?

What would you most certainly want to do before you die?

Something to do daily:

Something to do weekly:

Something you have always wanted to learn:

As you may notice, these questions help to take away the most obvious barriers that stand between you and your dream, one by one.

Your answers to these questions indicate where your passion lies, what gives you energy and what is truly important to you. That is where you should go in order to realize your dreams!

Daniëlle (37) wanted to live in a warm country, free from the routines she knew in The Netherlands. However, she did not want to do this by herself, and a broken relationship seemingly put an end to her emigration plans. In spite of this, she left the country and met the love of her life; a Colombian, in Miami. A few years later her dream became reality: she is married and has a beautiful daughter. However, living and working abroad does have a few drawbacks.

My natural wake up time is at a quarter pas nine. In the Netherlands I had to get up at seven every day. A nightmare. When I got to my work and had things to do it was fine, but my biological clock was simply confused. I did not enjoy the climate in the Netherlands, either. The weather was often cold, dark and gray. The combination with work from nine to five at a government institution did not make me happy. I wanted to leave. I wanted to go somewhere with a warm climate and more freedom. But I did not want to do this by myself.

When my then boyfriend set out to return to Israel, his home country, and asked if I wanted to join him, I did not have to think twice. I started taking Hebrew classes and quit my job. However, a few weeks before our departure, we broke up...
Bye bye dream. There I was. No boyfriend, no job, my house already rented out.

Since I had already taken the first step towards leaving the Netherlands, I persevered. Disappointed, love sick and frustrated, I went to my father in Miami. From there I made a few trips to South America.

And in Miami I chanced upon a really wonderful Colombian! Leonardo had spent ten years working as an engineer in New York and had just moved to Miami. He didn't know anybody there yet. He is a real meat-eater and was heading for the steakhouse, when he saw me sitting at a crêpe bar. While he has nothing with crêpes, he felt a strong attraction and he sat down next to me. We got to know eachother and felt a real click. I am a vegetarian, so we are an odd couple when it comes to food. And yet, things are great between us.

Wedding in Bogotá

One year later Leonardo and I live together in Miami and now we are married. The wedding was in Colombia. Many people are misinformed and afraid of Colombia. You only hear stories about drugs and guerrillas, but it is a very beautiful, developed country with friendly people. And Colombia is cheaper than the Netherlands or Miami, so we could marry with much more luxury for a smaller budget.

Twice I stayed with Leonardo's parents in Bogotá in order to organize everything. The first time I didn't even know these people and yet they welcomed me to their house for a whole month! They were very friendly; and the planning of a wedding is a good way to really get to know each other.

The same goes for my husband and me. True to my Dutch nature I wanted to plan every detail ahead, so I would be able to relax and enjoy the days surrounding the wedding. He, however, used the last days to plan all sorts of things. This caused some stressful moments... I call it a cultural difference; he says it has nothing to do with culture, but with personality.

Back to reality

Back in Miami, we returned to 'normal' life. Leonardo had a busy job and I was trying to get settled, organize a visa and think of a productive way to spend my days. In order to work as a children's psychologist I needed a work permit and proper licenses. Until I managed to sort those out, I temporarily helped my father (who is a realtor)

renting out apartments. This was not my schooling or field of experience, but it did give me a lot of freedom and flexibility.

Meanwhile, my biggest dream came true. I gave birth to a beautiful daughter. Zarah is my little princess and I enjoy her presence every day. However, motherhood can be quite demanding and sometimes lonely; especially during the first few months.

It is not easy to meet new people in Miami. Everyone works long, hard days and has little time to spare. Distances are bigger, too, which means spontaneous visits are out of the question.

It therefore took a little bit longer to make new friends. Now I get to know some other mothers through meetup groups. I've taken up volunteer work for 'Spirituality for kids'. This involves teaching important life-tools to children in schools. I've also followed courses in the local Kabbalah Center. Here, too, I met interesting people.

Most of my friends come from Colombia and other South American countries. Contact with Americans is much more superficial.

Financial uncertainty

While I started working in real estate to keep myself occupied, at some point I began taking it more seriously. I obtained a certificate as an estate agent, and now I have my own clients. This has actually turned out quite well for me: I now have many returning clients and referrals from existing clients. This keeps me rather busy.

This kind of work is easily combined with Zarah. As a baby she would simply come with me when I was showing a house. Everyone knows her: the tenants, the clients, the realtors. I always introduce her as 'my colleague'. Now Zarah has become a little older and won't sit in the stroller anymore, I hired a babysitter who helps me out for a few hours.

Being an estate agent, I meet all sorts of fun people and I earn money at the same time. However, the problem is that the real estate market in the US has completely collapsed. There's hardly any sales, only rental. This means more work and less profits. So this job keeps me off the streets and covers a part of my expenses, but I can't live off it.

My savings from the Netherlands are running out. Thankfully I've been able to rent out my apartment in the Netherlands; this covers a part of my costs, here. However, each time the tenant leaves it's difficult to find another tenant, considering the bad Dutch housing market...

Maybe Leonardo and I will want to go to Colombia for a while, some-day, or to another place that Leonardo might be sent by his business as an expat engineer. However, when we bought our apartment in Miami, times were different. Our mortgage is now higher than the market value of our house, which means we won't be able to sell it, should we wish to leave.

These are all insecurities that I must learn to live with, but it doesn't sit well with me that I have no control over my finances.

Visa

Of course I knew it would be difficult to get a visa for the US. Des-pite expensive lawyers, stacks of papers, translated diplomas, let-ters of recommendation and the passing of two years, it still did not work out. Each time I seem to be very close, and then there is a new procedure, an unfounded rejection or yet another setback. It's costing me a lot of money, time and energy. I was especially frustrated because I came to America on a tourist visa and had to leave the country every three months. Every time I had to pass immigration at the airport, my nerves caused a lot of stress. Had the immigration service found that I actually lived here, I would have been in trouble.

Thankfully Leonardo recently officially became an American, which means I can now get a visa as his wife.

In hindsight, all these steps that appeared to lead nowhere did turn out to be useful. In the end all my visa requests have bought me time; I did not have to leave the country every three months during my pregnancy. Meanwhile, I gathered the right documents in order to work as a certified psychologist. And my temporary real estate work has given Zarah a stable first year of her life. If I had started working as a psychologist I would have been away from home much more, and I could not have taken her with me like I do now.

Conclusion

I realized that the warm weather in Miami is not only pleasant. Sometimes it is simply too warm. Most of the time, life takes place inside, in the air conditioning. It does look nice outside with the sun and the palm trees. And sometimes I go to the beach; more often than in the Netherlands, at least.

In hindsight, I can say that leaving the Netherlands has absolutely done me good. I found the love of my life here and I am incredibly happy with our little daughter. I came to realize that the problems, worries and rut of daily life also apply to life in a warm country. It costs more time and creativity, but in the end we do manage to work things out. I am convinced of that.

Not everything may go according to your plans,
But in the end still work out for the better.

Be realistic. Or maybe not?

When you phrase your dream, do check if it is realistic. But be sure not to do this for too long.

For example, anyone will tell you it is not realistic to dream of becoming a top sportsman or a pop star when you're almost fifty years old. But think of the forty-nine-year-old Scottish singer Susan Boyle; her participation in Britain's Got Talent instantly made her world famous. Exceptions may confirm the rule, but they also show that everything is possible!

Search YouTube for 'Susan Boyle audition' and check her touching first public appearance.

On YouTube you will also find a rather old (and therefore funny) video of a world record attempt to build a complete house in two hours. Something that appears to be impossible is being realized in front of your eyes. Search for 'world record 2 hour house'.

Setting up Coins for Care did seem an unrealistic and impossible goal. At the introduction of the euro I wanted to collect all leftover foreign coins for charity, but I had no experience, contacts or budget. If I had conformed to the 'rules' for what is achievable, I would have never started. And yet I did and collected $25 million for charity! Don't let other people's notions of what is or isn't realistic hold you back.

There's another YouTube video to prove the point. In 'The Ball Girl' you can see how, at a baseball match, a ball is hit so far that everyone considers it 'out': the commentator of the match, the audience and even the catchers in the field, who make absolutely no effort to catch the ball. And suddenly someone runs and climbs against the walls of the stadium and catches the ball, after all! And it doesn't turn out to be one of the players; it's...the ball girl! She saw an opportunity where others weren't even watching anymore. What's more, she was already running when the rest had already concluded that the ball would be out. The chance was one in a million. She must have trained long and hard in order to be able to make a move of this kind. And she was in the right place at the right moment. A video of less than fifty seconds that leaves a lasting impression. Long live the ball girl! She teaches us that you can reach remarkable results when nobody has any expectations of you.

See what is achievable for you and dream a bit extra for good measure. If YOU don't believe it is possible, it will never happen.

Don't tell me the sky is the limit, when there are footprints on the moon.

At some point during our Caribbean sailing trip, we came to the island Saba. It is a dormant volcano and from the sea, it looks like a great rock; an uninviting stone wall.
It is remarkable how people can (and want to!) live on this rock. There is hardly a single flat piece of land, it is completely isolated and access from the sea is extremely difficult. Yet, it is home to about 1500 people.
From time immemorial, imported goods had to be lifted on the shoulders of strong men who would be immersed to their waists into the sea. They had to ascend no less than 524 steps that were hewn out of the cliffs. Everything on the island arrived in this way, including building materials, a piano and even, at some point, a bishop. The village on the other side of the island is called Hell's Gate, because it was an awful job to get supplies all the way out there, across small tracks.

So, the people of Saba wanted a real road. But engineers from the Netherlands said it was impossible; in some locations the angle was too steep for building a road. But the inhabitants of Saba are truly persistent. A man called Josephus Lambert Hassel decided to follow a correspondence (!) course in road construction, and in the year 1938, Saba inhabitants started building their road. It took no less than five years before the first part was finished and another three years before the first car arrived on the island. They dotingly call it 'the road that couldn't be built'. At some points it is so steep that a full car with four people cannot ascend!

The same goes for Saba's airport. Since there is hardly a flat piece of ground on the island, everyone said that an airport was out of the question. Rémy de Haenen, an enthusiastic pilot from the neighboring island of St Barts, said that he would try to land on a somewhat flat piece of land of just over four hundred yards. Together, the people of Saba cleared a runway and leveled it. The pilot landed and so, since 1959 Saba has an airport. It is the shortest commercial runway in the world. Pilots must follow a special training in order to land on Saba and it has even become a tourist attraction!

Does your dream seem impossible? The greater the challenge!

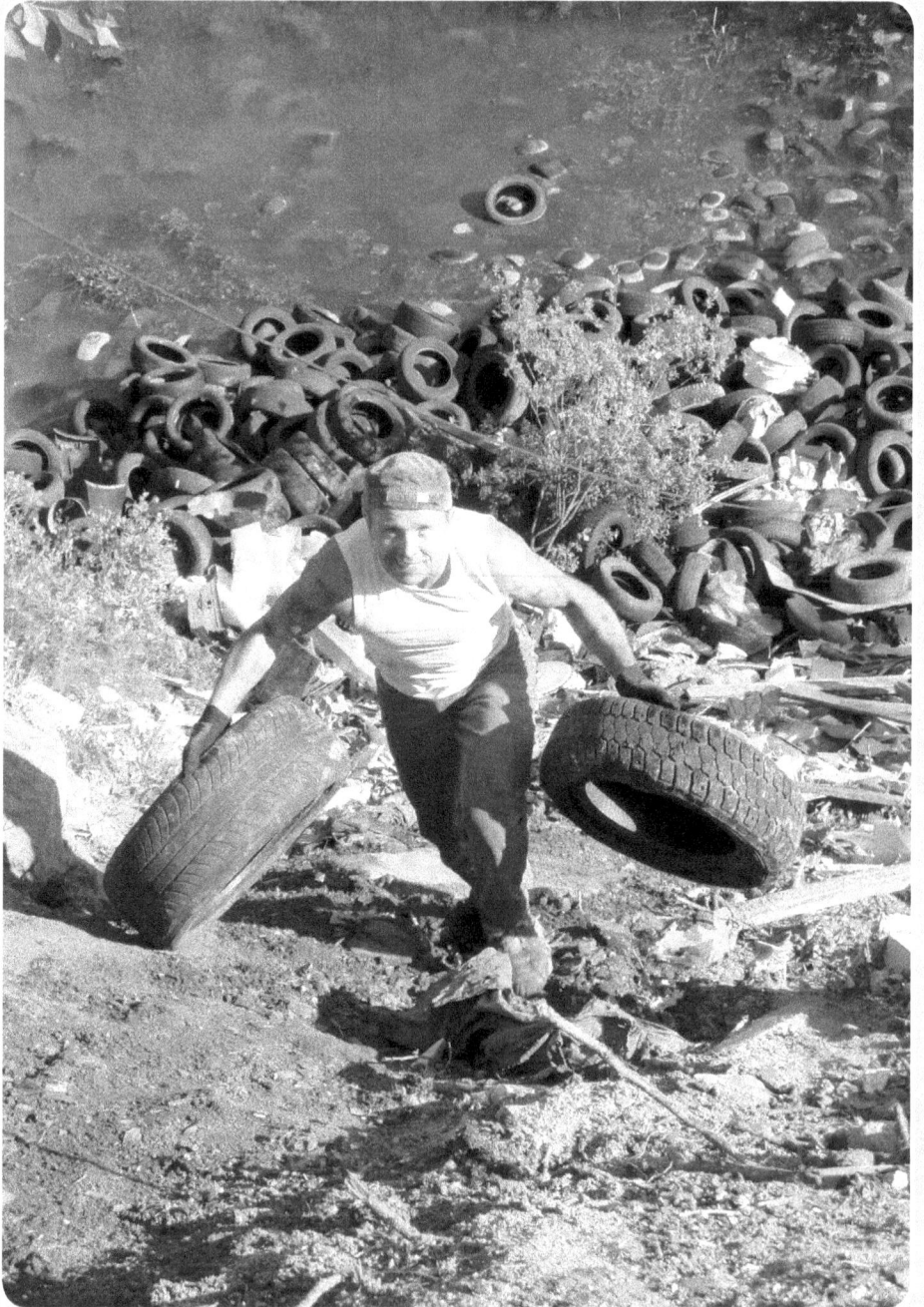

Rainer (43) felt scandalized by the illegally dumped trash in the forests of his home country, Estonia. In 2008, he initiated 'Let's do it!': a campaign to clean up the country in a single day, with the help of tens of thousands of volunteers. Today, the initiative is successful in multiple countries.

I am a bit of a loner and I love taking long walks in the forest. It is incredible what people dump in our forests: car tires, fridges and chemical waste. Every time I see this it angers me, but I thought there was nothing I could do. One day I was talking to a friend about my frustration, and he said, 'I have a dream: that one day, Estonia will be clean.' We visualized how beautiful this would be, but it seemed so unrealistic. However, he persisted: let's at least give it a try. He suggested cleaning up the country in five years, but this didn't feel good. In my impatience I wanted to clean the country in a single day. 'Let's make some kind of national holiday out of it,' I suggested. This was the start.

Carefully I introduced the idea of a cleanup day to some friends. I was surprised that they did not immediately reject the idea of cleaning up other people's waste! After a while we had a team of twenty people who all wanted to work on this project. At a given moment there were 600 volunteers. We realized that we were not capable of doing this by ourselves, so we tried to get experts and opinion leaders to think along with us. Journalists, computer programmers, technical experts, charities, politicians, sportsmen; even the president joined our campaign.

But we had no idea how much waste was out there. Each weekend we would try to map illegal garbage dumps together with our teams of volunteers. One Sunday I was walking in a forest, alone, and I called our little office to ask how many teams were active that day. 'You're the only one,' they said. At that moment I really just wanted to stop. What's the use when you are trying to change the whole country, all by yourself? It wasn't just about getting rid of garbage; a mentality shift had to take place. But still I couldn't stop. That day, in the forest, between the piles of garbage, I felt a pang in my heart. If I stop now, I'll never forgive myself, I decided, and I continued. The next weekend there were more teams at work, and the weeks that followed even more people helped.

Nobody had ever done what we wanted to do. Nobody had even thought that it might be possible. We had calculated that under normal circumstances, it would take the government three years and 32 million dollars to make this happen. We wanted to do it in one day, and pretty much without a budget! We had initiated the biggest media campaign ever in Estonia. Without spending a penny. On national television and on the radio, famous Estonians, sportsmen and politicians explained how important they thought this campaign and called on everyone to join in.

There was much to organize: Sorting trash is not a common practice in Estonia; we'd have to teach people how to do it. All trash would have to be collected and recycled after it had been sorted. We made deals with various recycling businesses for car tires, old furniture, chemical waste, and so on. We asked so many businesses for help that at some point they said, 'you're just like the mafia. We can't say no to you!'

We had calculated that we needed around forty thousand volunteers to remove all trash from the forests in one day. Two weeks before the planned date, ten thousand people had signed up. We didn't know if we would make it. But from that moment we couldn't do much more than wait and hope the fire would spread.

On the day of the cleanup I left my house early and saw many people in the streets. A neighbor and her son were wearing some kind of army clothes. Strange, I thought. Then it suddenly hit me that they were going to the cleanup! I realized that all people in the streets at that early hour were all heading to their designated cleanup spots. The whole country was in motion! This moved me. I could hardly believe it. Within twenty minutes we were out of stock of garbage bags. In the end, fifty thousand people came to help, and in one day, we cleared ten thousand tons of trash! International media had followed our campaign and this gave our country and the volunteers an enormous boost.

Extraordinarily, Estonia is still clean. Now and again a small pile of garbage is found and we clean it up. Clean-Up Day is now a yearly event. In the past, trash in the forest was normal. Now it is something to be ashamed of.

Our neighboring countries, Latvia and Lithuania, heard about our success and did not want to stay behind, of course. It became a kind of competition who could get the most people involved. Latvia got a hundred thousand people together and Lithuania even a hundred and ten thousand. It was such an enormous success that there simply wasn't enough trash for all those people! Next, Slovenia followed. This country has two million inhabitants, of which more than 271,000 took part in the cleanup campaign. That is thirteen percent of the population! This would equal 40 million people in the USA!

So far, these were all Eastern European countries. When I got a phone call from Portugal that they also wanted to join, I was surprised. 'It isn't dirty there, is it?' I thought. After Portugal I was asked by Brazil, and now there is even a campaign in India. Of all places!

It is unbelievable what my original idea has triggered. I have discovered that people are usually asked to take action against something: think demonstrations, strikes, and so on. But they really only get enthusiastic when they can take action for something. This creates a great sense of unity. It changed me, personally, too. To be honest, I wasn't really such a good person. I had a difficult childhood and a difficult life. I was an alcoholic. I am ashamed of who I was. But since this campaign I experience so much warmth from people. I have so many friends. I haven't had a drop of alcohol since.

I hope to inspire people with this story. It is really possible to clean up a country in a single day; not only trash in the forests, but also garbage in the hearts of people. If you initiate something like this, I must warn you: it will change you. Prepare to be changed. It is such a beautiful feeling!

Check out the YouTube video of this campaign. Search for 'Let's do it Estonia'.

The latest updates and plenty of inspiration can be found on the website of the worldwide campaign: www.letsdoitworld.org.

Rainer's tips:

Dare to dream! Nothing is impossible.

It all starts by sharing your dream with others.

Keep your team open: everyone can join in and be present at all meetings.

Don't exclude anyone; even if a business insists on exclusivity. We made no distinction between small or big sponsors; everyone's name was added to the same list.

Ask everyone to think along. We invited journalists into our team instead of sending out a press release. This helped them understand what we were trying to achieve, so they were able to think of ways to bring the message across and set the mentality shift in motion.

Make a plan!

Is something holding you back? Pretend it doesn't exist and make a hypothetical plan. This may help you cross the threshold. Solutions will follow naturally.

Do you think the step is too big? Imagine that you have already made the choice and are setting out, whatever your dream may be. Make a plan! What do you need? How will you go about it? Whom can you ask for help? What should you organize, learn, buy, ask, look up and so on? Often, these lists make the project more concrete and manageable. If something is well-structured, it makes it easier to take that step.

Hilda and Bas (page 46) experienced this first hand when they were dreaming of a Caribbean sailing trip. They shared how difficult it was to let go of their comfortable lives and begin their dream journey. When they made a hypothetical plan, the journey suddenly started taking shape. They thought of which islands they would want to visit, checked out nautical charts, made lists of what they should bring, what they should organize, and so on. Meanwhile they had wet their appetites to such an extent that they simply decided to go.

During a speech I once asked my audience about their dreams. A man with greying hair said that he would love to own a farm in Italy someday. I estimated him around sixty years of age. 'When would you like to have that farm?' I asked. He doubted. 'It'll never happen,' he answered, 'it's too expensive'. I enquired about the price tag of such a farm and was surprised to find out he had never actually checked any prices. Of course a dream will always stay out of reach this way. After my speech the man actually started looking things up online, and found that it is much cheaper than he always thought. Now he could make a concrete plan for saving money, check out farms with local realtors while on vacation, and within a few years, he would realize his dream!

exercise

EXERCISE map your dreams

Part 1:

Make an overview of what you would like to have, be and do. Include a deadline.

Under 'have' you write down what you would like to have; for example, a beautiful house, your own business, or a new mountain bike. Don't be ashamed! If you can't dream it, it will never become real!

Under 'be' you name who and what you would like to be; for example, a famous singer, a good mother or a business owner. For most things you would like to be, you will first need to do something. Write behind each 'be'-item what you'll have to do for it. For example, follow singing lessons, sign up for American Idol, read books on raising children, take business classes, and so on.

Then under 'do' continue writing what you would really like to do. Make a trip around the world? Learn how to sail, dance or paint? Speak a foreign language? Visit former classmates? First, make a list of everything you can think of. Afterwards, you circle the five most important items; the items that give you most energy.

In .... months/years I want to:

Have
-
-
-

Be	Do
-	-
-	-
-	-

A vision without action is a daydream.
Action without a vision is a nightmare.

Part 2:

For each of your five most important dreams, note at least five to do items. Things you must do in order to realize your dreams or make a step in the right direction. If it is a long-term plan, spread the to do items across a timeline. What must you do this week, this month, this year? And what next?

Dream 1:

To do item   Deadline

-

-

-

-

-

Dream 2:

To do item   Deadline

-

-

-

-

-

Dream 3:

To do item	Deadline
-	
-	
-	
-	
-	

Dream 4:

To do item	Deadline
-	
-	
-	
-	
-	

Dream 5:

To do item	Deadline
-	
-	
-	
-	
-	

Part 3:

It helps to share your dreams, resolutions and to do items. Find a buddy with whom you discuss what you have written down, and ask him or her to remind you of your deadlines. A buddy can be your partner, a family member or friend, a colleague, neighbor or acquaintance. Maybe your buddy also has dreams you can help him or her achieve in this way?

You'll see that your dreams can become much more concrete like this, and that it generates a lot of energy.

Two dreams!
For more than a year, Hilda (33) and Bas (36) sailed with their daughter (then two years of age), and their son (then eight months old) to and through the Caribbean. When they returned home they started their own business.

Our son couldn't even walk yet when we began our sailing trip. You're very conscious of the uncertainties: what are the risks we subject ourselves and our children to? Will the kids enjoy it? What if something serious happens to them along the way; will we ever be able to forgive ourselves? What if someone at home gets seriously ill when we're at sea for a prolonged period of time?

For a while already, we'd had a vague wish to spend some time away, with fair weather, on the water. Friends of ours had spent a year sailing and we thoroughly enjoyed their stories. At the same time, it was out of the question that we would ever give up our interesting jobs and cozy existence in the Netherlands. Hilda also felt that she first had to achieve something carreer wise before she would deserve such a trip. This way, the plans never became tangible.

Then, we decided to turn it into a hypothetical project, with lists of wishes and requirements and an estimated budget. 'Say, we were to go. What would we do and how would we go about it?' If you chop such a project into pieces and articulate it into concrete points of action, it actually becomes quite coherent. Then came the realization: we'll just do it, and soon! It felt like a kind of momentum that we needed to gain. Everything fell into place; postponement would turn into abandonment.

We both took navigation classes and we followed a medical course at Rotterdam's famous harbor medical center.

We got in touch with a friendly doctor who would assist us via radio during our trip, if needed. We learned the most essential things for when you're at sea for a few weeks. For example, stitching wounds: we practiced on a chicken leg...

Before we knew it, the day of departure had come. It was quite emotional to say goodbye to family and friends for a whole year. It was therefore extra special when they visited us during our trip. These shared vacations were an enormous bonus. How often do you get to travel with your parents or good friends? Nobody can take away the memory of these special weeks.

We experienced incredible things. For example, at some point in the Bay of Biscay the wind dropped completely. Just before we wanted to turn on the engine, we saw a whale. The sea was completely calm; the whale, stately and at ease, circled the boat, now and then blowing out air. What an incredible mighty sight! It was almost too exciting, because the whale stayed close to the boat for quite a while. We hoped he wouldn't fall in love with our beautiful dark fin keel. When the whale finally disappeared into the depths of the sea, we breathed a sigh of relief.

We were going to commence our long crossing to the Caribbean from the Canary Islands. The three-week ocean crossing we sailed with a group of 220 other boats. When, at last, we left Las Palmas, the whole wharf was filled with waving people. It was an unbelievable feeling when we slowly sailed from the harbor, heading out to the other side of the Atlantic Ocean.

Our initial worries about how Lisanne and Sem would release their excess energy while we were at sea proved unnecessary. The lack of space was compensated with a lot of creativity. Swinging, swaying and even pole-dancing; it was all possible on the boat.

After exactly three weeks at sea we arrived at St Lucia. We were very relieved and thankful that everything went well. Somewhat befuddled, we searched for the stowed-away ropes and buffers, which we hadn't used for so long. Friends were awaiting us on the wharf, waving, rum punch ready for us; delicious!

In the Caribbean we visited beautiful places; each island was even more stunning than the previous. When we arrived at Horseshoe Reef we were speechless. It was truly more beautiful than a postcard. We were anchored in the middle of the uninhabited Bounty islands, in a sort of mega tropical swimming pool. There was nothing there, but we had everything: each other and the boat. We produced our own electricity with the generator, we had cold drinks and delicious food on board. For days we lived on the white beach and in the light-blue water.

On the volcanic island of Dominica, a guide named Maclin took us on a private tour. The land there is so fertile that nobody has to go hungry. Our guide showed us where and how mango, pineapple, papaya, dasheen, yam, grapefruit, tea, thyme and bay leaves grow. We realized how far removed from nature we usually live. We were invited to pick our own super fresh fruits and prepare freshly-picked tea.

On the tiny Les Saintes islands, something completely unexpected happened. In a supermarket we suddenly felt an enormous shock. Products fell off the shelves. Sem awoke in his stroller with a cry, and we automatically huddled over the children. We realized that we had to hurry outside. Once there, again we felt major shocks. There was panic; everyone walked away from the buildings while calling on their phones. Scared, we returned to our boat. For a year we had lived mostly on the water, where we had feared completely different dangers, but now, on land, we experienced an earthquake (5.3 on the Richter scale). This danger came totally unexpected. We quickly sailed on, in search of more solid ground beneath our keel. We hope to never experience this again.

During our temporary sailor's lives we met a surprising amount of interesting people. It is very special that all sailors have time to spare. There are no agendas, no appointments. You approach each other by dinghy (a small rubber boat), and frequently, you come across unexpected moments of fun. If it clicks you'll seek each other in the next bay, and this way, you quickly make special contacts.

Just to poke fun at stressed life in the western world: on Monday mornings we had extensive 'meetings' with the crew of other boats that were anchored nearby, while treading water. Points on the agenda: what shall we do this afternoon?, what is the next destination?, a report of radio contact with other boats, general questions and whatever else may need to be discussed. Naturally, we closed the meeting with a cup of coffee on the afterdeck.

After a year in the Caribbean and yet another long Atlantic crossing, we were on our way back to Europe. It was time that our tight-knit family would detach a little. This was not easy, after thirteen months of doing everything with the four of us. However, Lisanne immediately wanted to sleep over at Granny and Granddad's. Beaming, she asked, 'and you won't come along?' It was suddenly very quiet on the boat. Lisanne also really loved the notion of going to kindergarten. 'Then you'll drop me off and you won't be allowed to stay, right?' she asked with hope. Life is hard for soft hearted parents.

One morning we saw the Dutch harbor town of IJmuiden in the distance. A year ago, this was the place where friends and family waved us goodbye, excited and uncertain about what the year would bring us. Unbelievable that we were here, again; a year filled with positive experiences behind us. To celebrate, we raised the flags of all the countries we had visited. And there they were, our most loyal fans, cheering on the wharf. A very emotional moment; we were unable to hold back our tears.

Ultimately, the trip was fantastic. We proved a strong team: of one mind, balanced, and having a lot of fun and joy. The trip brought us new friends and even a closer bond with 'old' friends and family, who were involved and interested in us, tried, stimulated and supported us, visited us, and were there for us when we returned home.

We have learned to seize moments of joy. When traveling, you are quite busy 24 hours a day. Tending to the children (no babysitters, no grandparents around), fixing the boat (there's always something to repair and all sorts of normal things such as arranging for water and electricity take more time than on land) and of course enjoying the trip itself.

Child's Play
Our biggest concern before our departure was the children. Would this work out all right? Is a journey like this fit for children? We thought we probably wouldn't come across many other small children on other boats. Nothing is less true. Frequently there was a complete stroller parade on the beach.

The trip really went wondrously well. Traveling with children also gives rise to special experiences. You will look at things from a completely new perspective.

> **Interesting things the kids said:**
> *'My best friend Tom lives on an island called Amsterdam.'*
> **After returning to the Netherlands:**
> *'Does everyone here live in a house?'*
> *'When will we leave again?'*

New dreams

Ever since the trip we have much more confidence in following big and small dreams. Starting our own business was quite a well-organized venture compared to our sailing trip. Here we would not come across any life threats (storm, shipwrecking, and so on); we would simply risk financial setbacks.

Meanwhile, we knew that we could easily (temporarily) live off a small budget. And, more importantly, we had and have a firm conviction that this plan, too, can succeed.

The idea for Tapas Club was formed during our travels: often our glass of wine was accompanied by all sorts of local bites to eat. We believed that by bringing these authentic specialties to the Netherlands, we could also bring back a bit of that feeling. It wasn't easy to set up the business, but slowly this started to get going: caterers, delicacy shops, and restaurants are all enthusiastic about our authentic little dishes.

A few years down the road it has been fun to find out that what looked like a dream then – to start our own business – has become reality. Tapas Club has conquered a place on the Dutch market. It is an exciting challenge to expand our business and, within this context, realize new (smaller) dreams. This year we are aiming for the Belgian market; going south is the new dream, also business wise.

With this dream, everything falls into place: we're doing what we're good at and what makes us happy. We're combining our passion for good food with our experiences at large food businesses and the wish to flexibly and creatively fill in our work and working schedule.

It is unusual to give up your job twice, not because you are not enjoying yourself or because you have a better alternative, but because you want to take some time doing nothing work more flexible and location independent. Again, this forced us to make choices and seize opportunities. In the worst-case scenario, if it wouldn't work out, we would have to get back to searching for 'normal' jobs. During the startup phase we took turns working part-time as freelancers for large corporations in order to earn a bit of extra money.

The first year we could hardly go on vacation because the work just continued and we couldn't leave it to anybody else. By organizing things differently and by making optimal use of technological developments, we managed to work more flexible and location independent. By now we're able to work from anywhere without our clients noticing. All we need is the internet and a mobile phone. Apart from that, our (free lance) employees can easily work from home to solve a problem, if needed. This way, it quickly became possible to go on a trip without any problems, for example to seek out new products or simply go on a long, stress-free vacation. This means that dream-trips are still possible and our dream to live in Spain for a few months to work from there is getting closer.

We are continuously searching for smart solutions, also if they are unusual or new. Because we started our business from scratch, we were free to choose an ideal form. We work as a business networking organization, which means we are more flexible and decisive than old economy organizations.

After having worked for years as employees of large corporations, it was quite a challenge to deal with the many uncertainties of entrepreneurship. In the beginning, being your own boss mostly means financial uncertainty, hard work and having to organize everything yourself. There is no boss or management team you can blame; you chose this yourself. You'll come across deep lows that are, thankfully, compensated by many more highs. When we feel insecure, we try to think of the worst thing that could happen. If things go wrong, in the worst case we may have to spend some time living off very little money or do some less interesting work. This helps us put feelings of insecurity into perspective. We can imagine worse things happening.

We learned a lot. By starting your own business, you are forced to develop yourself in many fields. In the beginning you do almost everything yourself: from operations to strategy to finance and administration. We sometimes joke that it is the perfect applied MBA course.

Keep on dreaming...
The sailing trip was actually our first great dream that we consciously chose to pursue and had to overcome barriers for. This has turned out to be a super experience and it gives us the confidence we need to pursue other dreams.

Life is never exactly what you want it to be. For example, you can't choose your health or the health of your loved ones. This is something so feeble, and so we try to enjoy every moment in life. While it often doesn't feel like it, you can influence many things in your life. Your own choices determine your fortune as well as that of the people around you. It is possible to do things differently or change them. When you realize this, much is possible, and there is hope in dreaming.

We noticed it's not only about realizing dreams, but especially about enjoying dreaming and following dreams. It is a challenge to not only look ahead, but simply rejoice in the small steps that you take today in the desired direction, and in the new insights, special encounters and experiences that your steps bring.

**Each day, each second is an opportunity
to realize a small or a big dream.
The trick is to find out what your dreams are and
what makes you happy.
It is even trickier to seize this
happiness and enjoy it.**

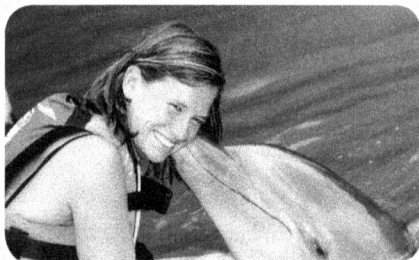

Tips from Hilda and Bas:

Pretend you made the decision today to follow your dream, and make a plan. Put it in writing and make it as concrete as possible, with action points, requirements, time planning and a budget. It is fantastic to do this and, bit by bit, you'll get closer to realizing your dream. This way, you take a gradual decision to go or not go for it, which makes it a lot easier.

Always grant yourself the freedom to adjust your dream along the way or exchange it for another one. This freedom of choice gives you peace of mind and it can also keep bringing you new, exciting experiences.

Following your dreams generates a lot of energy. The attempt alone can deeply satisfy you. Enjoy the ride as well as the destination!

If a barrier appears to be insurmountable, it can be a challenge to think about it creatively and approach it with an open mind. While it may not always appear so, many things are in your own hands and a solution may come unexpectedly.

Something to ponder...

A rich businessman on vacation in Mexico stumbles upon a fisherman napping lazily by his boat.

'Why aren't you fishing?' the businessman asks.

'Because I have caught enough fish for today,' the fisherman says.

The businessman suggests that the fisherman could catch a few more.

'What would I do with them?' the fisherman thinks aloud.

'You could earn more money,' was the answer. 'With it, you could install an engine on your boat so you could take your boat further onto the sea and catch more fish. Then you could earn enough money to buy nylon nets. These could bring you even more fish and more money. Soon enough you'd have enough money to own two boats...maybe a whole fleet. Then you wouldn't have to sell to a middleman; you could supply directly to the factory. Then you would be a rich man, like me,' the businessman explains triumphantly.

'Why would I want that?' the fisherman asks, again.

'Because then you could truly enjoy life and do what you really want.'

'And what do you think I'm doing right now?' the fisherman concludes as he slides his hat back over his face, resuming his siesta.

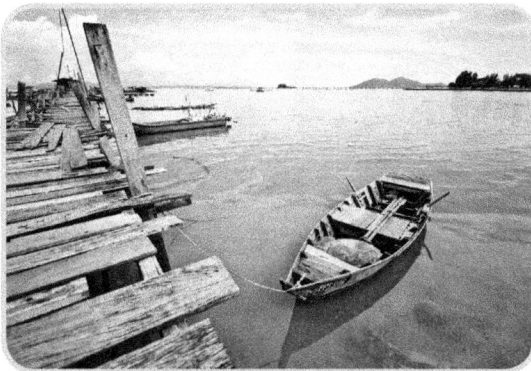

Look beyond your goal

Some time ago, during a karate workshop, I learned to split a block of concrete with my bare hands. Of course you have to hold your hand in a certain way, so you don't hurt yourself. And you have to hit the block in the exact middle, where there is least tension. And you have to concentrate and believe you can do it. But the most important tip I got before I, too, managed to split such a big, gray, hard block, was this: don't aim for the block itself, but look beyond your goal. Focus on a point behind the block of concrete and direct your hand there. If you aim for the block, when you reach it you'll be at the end of your blow where it loses its strength. If you focus beyond the block, your blow has the most speed and strength at the moment that your hand passes the block of concrete 'by chance'. It felt completely absurd to give it a try. But because I aimed beyond the block and focused on that point, I hardly noticed that my hand had split the concrete in two![4]

You can apply this eastern philosophy in other situations, too.

Thanks to www.ribbersbrick.com

For example, many people think that money is the solution and therefore dream of a large sum of it. However, if you focus on what you would ultimately like to do with that money, you will discover that there are usually also other ways to reach it.

Do you think you must first work really hard for a few years in order to save enough money, so you can then take it easy? Maybe you can work less already and simply adjust your spending habits. Then you can already enjoy your life now, just like the fisherman in the story.

Sylvia (page 62) thought that she wanted to sail, but although she still loves sailing, she discovered that what is really important to her is the sense of freedom that sailing gives her. This freedom she has now found in her new job.

Marnix (page 70) felt an uncontrollable need for freedom after his illness and his participation in Survivor. He considered leaving everything behind in order to travel. Fortunately he discovered that the combination of wanderlust, security and responsibility could also be found within his beloved family and his work.

Johanna (page 234) wanted to do development work in Africa. After a while she discovered that there were people in her immediate vicinity who could also use some support. Next to her job, she now helps with various projects in her own environment, through her church.

During my charity period I was approached by a group of people who wanted to collect money for a charity in Africa. I asked them what they would do with that money. 'We want to buy refrigerators for a local hospital,' they told me enthusiastically. They did experience fundraising as a stumbling block. There were so many charities asking for money. 'Maybe, instead of asking money from private individuals, it is easier to ask for refrigerators from a manufacturer,' I suggested. This worked! They now only had to ask one party, and without any time-consuming intermediary steps, they managed to reach their goal.

If you recognize this principle, you can help yourself or others by asking why you or they really want something, and what makes it so attractive.

Years ago, in the jungle of Suriname, I visited a tiny Maroon village. I still remember how, as I stepped out of the canoe that had taken me there, I saw school books and notebooks floating in the water. I asked my guide why this was, and he explained: 'The school year has just finished...' Apparently school was seen as a necessary evil and not held in high regard.

I was invited to visit the chieftain of the village and the guide would be the interpreter. After an exchange of formalities, I impulsively asked if there was something we could possibly help the chieftain with. 'I am not part of a relief organization,' I added, just to be sure, 'but I would like to get an idea of the problems that villages like yours may experience.'

The chieftain thought for a moment, and answered, to my surprise; 'we need a disco.' I didn't know what to say. We were in the middle of the jungle, the village clearly had all sorts of problems, and the chieftain, who had appeared to me as a sensible man, wanted a disco? I already visualized myself at a relief organization with such a request. Or imagine a fundraising campaign for this!

Still, I had a feeling that there was more to this. The chieftain talked about it with passion. On being asked, he explained, 'our biggest problem is that all youth are leaving the village in order to go to Paramaribo, where they have discos. If we build a disco, here, they may decide to stay.'

Now I knew the root of the problem, we could talk about what really mattered and about possible solutions.

A while ago I thought that I would really like to be in Oprah Winfrey's show. This seemed to be the ultimate opportunity to reach millions, stir them and wake them up. I focused completely on Oprah. When I heard that she would soon stop her show, I was devastated.

Until someone asked me, 'why did you want to be on Oprah's show, again?' Only then was I reminded that there are, of course, other ways to inspire people, and my eyes were opened. I had blinded myself on a 'means' instead of keeping my goal in mind.

exercise

EXERCISE:

Ask yourself what you truly want. Why do you want to achieve this? What's beyond it? What need do you aim to fulfill? And when you have reached this goal, then what? Is there another desire beyond it? And beyond that one?

Keep on asking yourself these questions until you know what you really truly want. Then think of the shortest route there.

Tip: sometimes it helps if another person asks you these questions and thinks along with you. Just like me, you may have a 'blind spot' for what is behind your dream or wish.

If, too quickly, you answer, 'this is it, there's nothing behind this,' then chances are that you have already blinded yourself by your dream and that you're no longer open to seeing what is truly behind it.

Sylvia (53): from sailing journey to spiritual coach for children.

My path has taken all sorts of unexpected turns. It started with my dream to make a sailing journey. Twenty years ago I had already sailed with my previous partner. After my divorce I started taking sailing seriously and I earned my diplomas.

The feeling of freedom sat very well with me. Sailing is a sporty, active hobby and I love it. Working together with the elements, playing with wind and water. The technical aspect, too, really appeals to me. How do you make optimal use of the wind and the current? Besides, I simply love being on and near the water.

Therefore, I sailed a lot the past few years: in the Netherlands, in Greece, and even around Svalbard. These were special experiences. I even considered buying a sailing boat, but I still haven't gotten to it.

The past two years I deepened my search as to where my heart is and what my purpose is on this earth. I realized that my need for freedom partially arose from my work in education, in which I actually felt a lack of freedom.

I feel that both I as well as the children can not really be who we are and live according to the impulses that come from within.

I have always searched for an alternative kind of education, with an idea and a vision behind it. With space and freedom for children. Not only a place where knowledge is imparted, but also where the total child is seen. I started with Jena Plan education and from there I switched to the Montessori method. But there, too, I felt an increasing amount of restrictions.

Time and time again I asked myself the question, 'where is my essence, my heart and my longing?'.

It has always fascinated me how indigenous people live, and how they deal with nature and with each other. How they think about development, healing and curing.

Because of two very special trips to England and Peru I have come into contact with Indians and shamans. Both times I allowed my intuition to guide me, and this resulted in many encounters, cere-monies and insights. Meanwhile I have further looked into the way of life and life visions of shamans. I have also received some hea-lings and initiations from various shamans.

Shamans use energy to work at transformation and healing, bringing a new kind of balance. They transform heavy energy to light energy, without judging anyone. There is no good or evil.

My desire is to be a shaman for children, in my own way. This is what touches the deepest core of my being and what I ultimately long for. Helping children, supporting them and guiding them to reach their hearts and stay true to themselves.

In the Dutch magazine *Educare* I read about a course for spiritual coaching for children: guiding children to their essence and helping them stay there. I have completed the course and I am now a cer-tified spiritual coach for children. This course has taught me how to give shape to my deepest desires. I now develop and give workshops.

Meanwhile I quit my job as a teacher at a Montessori elementary school. I want to work with children in a different way: much more from the center of the child; child-focused. I find their total develop-ment essential, not only their cognitive development. Where can a child's strengths and essence be found, and how can I, or the school, create space for a child to discover this, so they can remain true to themselves? It is so important that they can be true to themselves, and that their development can unfold in a natural way.

In my search for new kinds of education I visited many schools for natural learning. In one of them I worked for a year.

I am building my practice now: "Natuurlijk wijs kind" (natural wise child). I help children and sometimes together with the parents to find their own nature, their strength, their own wisdom and their passion. Feel a part of nature, mother earth. And respect all.

I am connecting with 'Challenge day'. I hope for myself to cooperate with this beautiful program to help young people and schools to feel connected to each other.

challengeday.org

I also want to investigate the possibility to start a small school myself.

Now, action must come completely from within me, and I experience this as a challenge. It's about believing in myself and following my heart and my passion. And I go with the flow.

And this is what matters most: to believe in yourself. Believe in the divine within you. I want to help children and adults with this belief. And myself as well, as you can read here.

Sylvia's tips:

I believe in a kind of guidance from above. And I frequently ask for signs that show me the way.

Be on the lookout for signs. Keep your eyes and ears open and see what comes by. If you are driven by the idea of something and you suddenly see or hear something about it, or if the same thing comes to your attention multiple times, this is a sign. Coincidences don't exist. Do something with it.

Follow your heart. What makes you happy? Take your desires seriously.

Now and again, seek out silence (nature, meditation or yoga), so that you can also 'hear' your own heart.

Listen to your body. Your body tells you the truth. Does your heart skip a beat or do you get a headache?

Take yourself seriously and show compassion for yourself. Treat yourself with tenderness.

Let go of expectations as much as possible. Do not judge; try to look at things that cross your path with childlike wonder.

If something just doesn't want to manifest, let it go and open yourself to something else.

Don't wait for the right moment

Everything is a choice, also refraining from choosing; be aware of this. Waiting until the children are older, until work is less busy, until you have saved enough money, until you or your partner retires, until you no longer have to take care of your parents, until you have found the right partner, and so on; there is always some reason or excuse why you should not yet do what you actually want to do. Realize that the perfect moment, where all circumstances are ideal, will never come! If you wait for this moment, your dream will never come true. Everyone who has pursued their dreams states that, at a given moment, they simply made the first step, and the rest just followed. All problems you can think of in advance can be overcome along the way.

When most people see an opportunity, they will stop to think and evaluate their chances before they may or may not proceed to action. In his newest book, Richard Branson embraces the philosophy, *Screw It, Let's Do It*. This attitude is characteristic for Richard's success.

Some people wait for the right moment to do something, others wait for the right moment to stop something. In both cases, the same rule applies. Do it NOW!

From idea to production and worldwide delivery in three days
Just after Apple had launched the iPad, Martijn Aslander (page 106) was playing with his new gadget. He thought it might be useful if you could rest it in a vertical position. The next day he went to visit seventy-five-year-old Simon and he explained his idea. Simon did not have an iPad, but he did have a tool shed. Within an hour he made a stand using a simple, wooden block. David, another friend, came by, took some pictures, and wrote a fun blog about the wooden iPad stand online. Two days later the news was had been picked up by the biggest technology website in the world: Wired. Other sites soon followed. To make a long story short: within a few days, orders from more than twenty countries came in. A friend took care of shipping the iPad stands, which only cost five dollars each.

This all unfolded simply by ACTING in the moment, and not by first organizing meetings, writing reports and doing research. The idea was created on a Friday afternoon; on Monday the first orders were shipped. Normally you would say this could never be done, but nowadays, partially thanks to social media, it is all possible. www.woodenipadstands.com

Jumping from a high-speed train

It was very difficult for me to stop with my volunteer work at the time. However hard I tried to involve others, the Donor Organization really revolved around me. Who would take over my work if I quit? I decided that I could only stop when I had found a replacement. But I did not succeed at finding someone who could and wanted to take over my more than fulltime, unpaid job. Then I decided that I would first transfer all the projects to sponsors. With some projects this worked, with others it didn't. I felt uncomfortable disappointing my interns, sponsors and partners by stopping. And yet everything pointed towards my departure. I no longer experienced any joy from my charity work, I showed signs of stress and I was overworked; I started suffering more and more ailments. Just when I decided to announce my leave, a huge sponsor arrived on the scene, who wanted to invest three hundred thousand euro in the coming three years. Of course I could not give up then...

Ultimately, money did not solve my problem: I just couldn't go on, I was done with charity and I wanted something else. My replacement was still nowhere to be found.

Health problems finally settled my decision to stop. The time would never be right, therefore I simply had to get it over and done with.

It felt like jumping off a high-speed train. It can't be done, it's not allowed, it is dangerous and everyone thinks you're crazy. You're standing by the open door of the train carriage. The outside world rushes by, while the wind hits your face. Against better judgment you do jump, by the mercy of God. You close your eyes and prepare yourself for the blow. Your body curls up and you roll and roll, completely disoriented, until you finally come to a halt. First you check to see if you're alive and well. works. Slowly you look around and you realize that you did it, and that the train, which symbolizes everything that drove you crazy, simply continues onward! You find yourself in a peaceful, new landscape, full of exciting opportunities and surprises!

I went before you and I can say: it feels completely unnatural at the moment that you have to make the jump, but afterwards you know that this was the only right thing that you could have done. There is a whole world outside of the train that you are never even aware of inside. I have no regrets! (Apart from the realization that I should have jumped much, much sooner...)

© Jeroen van Amelsvoort

Marnix (42) from Belgium survived cancer and then completely redesigned his life. He won *Survivor* and began traveling. In the end he found a balance between his new urge to travel, his old job and his beloved family.

Before I got sick I was mostly occupied with my job and my family. For my job at the Federal Judicial Police in Brussels I worked lots of overtime, and as it was two hours away from where I live, I spent four hours a day on the road. We also have three children and a busy family life. I never searched for a deeper meaning. You simply accept that all your time goes into your work and your family and there is not much space for other things.

In January 2004 I was diagnosed with testicular cancer. I had trouble realizing that I was really very sick. You hear about cancer occasionally, but it had never been prominent in my life; I simply never thought about it. And suddenly the illness was in my own body. When I got sick, I was overcome with fear that time was running out. There were still so many things that I wanted to do. Suddenly I realized that there is a limit to the amount of time you have; a limit to your life. At that moment I realized that I had to do something with my time and use it as well as I could. I am under the impression that many people don't even think about this.

That first month everything was uncertain. Everything revolved around the question: what are my chances to survive this? I thought that my life was over. I told my wife, 'Eventually you'll have to take care of the children by yourself. I will try to sort out all the practicalities for our family, while I still can.'

When the treatments started, hope returned. The chemotherapy seemed to catch on very well.

A five-year waiting period followed the treatments. I considered every minute as quality time. In the past I used to ask myself, 'how will I make it through this long day?' Now I asked, 'I want to do this, and this; how will I fit it all in a single day?' I had the feeling that I had lost time. I had spent so many years living unconsciously.

When you're sick, you're immobile; you can't take on another challenge. Everything you want to do is a dream, even the most normal things. As soon as you start feeling a little better, you therefore know: now is the time to do the things I always wanted to do. If I don't do them now, I'll never do them.

My vague, distant dream had always been to make a trip around the world; to take a sabbatical. Just to spend a period in my life to broaden my horizon and my mind without having to think about earning money. I dreamed about just doing 'my thing' for a while, without having to worry about any obligations.

Therefore the first thing I did when I was done with my treatments was to go on vacation. Less than two weeks after my last chemotherapy I headed off to Cuba, together with my wife and a good friend who is a nurse. We booked our flight a day in advance and my wife asked her boss if she could take time off on the spot. We felt as though we had just escaped! I was still bald and didn't have eyebrows. I had been in hospital for four months and suddenly there I was, on a pearly white beach, with blue water and a dazzling sun. After my struggle to keep my life, all of a sudden I was in control again. I felt energy coursing through my body. I was back, but felt like a different person. I used to live in a straight line, and from this moment onward I wanted everything raised to the square. This experience is very different, as well as its interpretation.

This is how I started traveling, and I haven't stopped since. After that trip I resumed my job. But one month later I was climbing Monte Perdido in Spain: the second highest mountain of the Spanish Pyrenees. My friend, the nurse, had taken along a bag of medicines, just in case.

Together we climbed to the summit of four thousand meters in two days. I felt great! If you can do that, two months after chemotherapy, you can conquer the world.

Before my illness I had signed up for the reality TV show *Survivor* three times already. Each time I had written a letter, like thousands of others, explaining, 'I have a family with children and I would like

The first step

The last picture of Marnix wearing a watch.
After his tipto Cuba he took it off, to never wear it again.

to take a break.' I never received a response. They get four thousand letters each year from people who would love to spend some time on a tropical island...

Now I took on the project with renewed energy. I wrote another letter, this time short and powerful. I told them I had been ill and continued:

I was selected for the program and departed for Malaysia not much later. There I spent two weeks in an abandoned cave and I won *Survivor* after seven weeks of hardships. Every test I did – such as an extreme swim from island to island – to me symbolized my victory over my illness. It was a personal journey of triumph. *Survivor* was a new start to me, a new beginning.

> 'As an ultimate test in life I want to shine again! I want to go the bitter end of abstinence and meet myself in barren circumstances. I want to redefine my limits. A few months ago this was in a fight without opponents; I should be able to repeat this...but this time against opponents who don't yet know the black hole that I have come out of...and I want to show them that you can achieve much if you are determined and if you believe in yourself.'

© Jeroen van Amelsvoort

Because I had been so sick and was now living a dream, the extremes were very far apart. Eleven months earlier I had been lying in a hospital bed, undergoing chemotherapy. A little later I was in Malaysia for the first time in my life, in a dream. The first days I didn't quite realize it. I simply let myself float along, feeling and experiencing the adventure. Together with Esther I lived in a cave, on a rock in the middle of the sea. We had absolutely nothing there, but we saw everything positively; we made the most of it. We took every moment as it came. It was an eye-opener. At a certain moment my vision on life changed.

This is how I learned to enjoy peace and quietude. I never used to make time for this. Doing nothing, a whole day. Absolutely nothing. How many people can say that they ever did nothing, a whole day long? Or that they spent time at a place where there is absolutely nothing to do? Then you simply have to live in the moment.

After two months I returned home and I had to resume ordinary life. The first months I was still floating along; my heart wasn't really in it. Others had to draw me back to reality. I had to work again; there were responsibilities at home and at work, but my mind shouted 'NO!' This was a strange feeling. I longed to continue the lifestyle I had in Malaysia. It was an enormous confrontation.

If it had been possible, I would have simply left. Taken a backpack and headed off for a few years. I had the feeling I wanted to devour the world; that's how greedy I was. Working simply wasn't my thing. I realized that I had to do it; everyone does, but my heart wasn't in it. I wanted to butter my bread on both sides. I wanted my family, but I did not want to be tied down. I did not want them to keep me from doing my thing. After six months I realized that the life I wanted to lead was not feasible. However, I did not resign myself to this. I wanted to travel; I wanted to experience things; I wanted more!

I managed to convince my wife, Carla, to let me take the children on a skiing vacation. I also spent a week in Ireland with some friends and I went on a music vacation for a few days. I went to Egypt for a week, by myself. Carla thought all of that wasn't really necessary, but I really needed those little outings, and much more frequently than she did. I simply needed to get away. Soon after, I disappeared to Nepal to spend a month trekking: I wanted to climb the Mount Everest trail as far as I could without any technical support. It wasn't simply vacation: I was seeking out a challenge. I was driven by an internal voice: 'if you don't do it now, tomorrow may be too late'.

Of course, this increasingly became a point of friction at home. In hindsight, Carla was very patient with me. She was good at letting me go, but when she eventually tried to rein me in again, it was already too late. This caused tension within the family. She wanted everything to become the way it used to be. But I couldn't change back to who I was before my illness, before *Survivor*.

It was as though my world had opened up and I couldn't close it down again.

In those times, Carla considered me a selfish person. I don't think I was, because I still fulfilled my duties as a father. I did what I could for the family, but I also wanted to do things for myself within the possibilities that I had. The problem was that I constantly wanted to expand my horizon.

Then Carla decided to come along! Together we traveled to the source of the river Ganges in India, at the foot of the Himalayas. It was the first time she ever went backpacking. We had some arguments. But she actually quite enjoyed herself. I thought, 'see, I'm not asking too much to do these kinds of things and have a family at the same time!' When I traveled through Nepal alone for a month, I had constantly felt guilt. Should I do this, may I do this? Now we traveled together, we had a good time together and I did not feel guilty; she, too, enjoyed the trip, after all.

In India with Carla

My new attitude towards life verges a lot of adaptability from Carla. She can enjoy my lust for life, as long as it's not too much. She will now take a month off work so we can go to South Africa together: a sign that she also enjoys these adventures and finds them important. She now gets energy from traveling. The children are a bit older and more independent, which gives us more space. We make a lot of trips together. For example, we went to Tuscany by motorcycle. Sometimes I go alone or with friends, or with my music mate; I need that for myself.

My illness has been a turning point. Especially in how I deal with time; there is this restless feeling that I don't have enough time. I want to seize every moment and don't think about the future. I decided to live without a calendar and stopped wearing a watch.

I still work for the same investigation unit, but I now research crimes related to drugs instead of human trafficking. I want to do something different every five years. If I feel that I'm working on autopilot, I will search for another challenge. I now work in an office only twenty minutes away from my home. I no longer work overtime and I therefore have much more time for my family and other social events.

It wasn't easy striking the golden mean. It took a few years. I went from a deep pit to an absolute climax, and it was difficult finding a balance after this. The more you live in extremes, the more you'll want to seek out your own boundaries. Sometimes you don't realize that you're going too far. At a given moment this will create so much tension within your relationships that someone will blow the whistle on you. Then I said to myself, 'Marnix, this is the situation you find yourself in; make the most of it, do whatever you can within your capabilities.' I have to work, but I try to enjoy it. When I am at home, I want to be there more intensely. Automatically, the violins tune themselves to each other. Carla can live with it; I can too. Now matters have found their course, and a lot of fun things are taking place.

What is Your Dream?

Tips from Marnix:

There are so many awesome things you can do! Don't be a lame duck; try to find a challenge that will make life meaningful to you. Everyone can do something, in their own way, that will give them satisfaction. This is the essence of being happy.

Live in the moment. Enjoy more intensely. Make the best of what you do every day: your work, your family; but try to be less dependent on them.

You must be aware of what you want and actually do it. Some people realize this, but don't take action. I may already have been living a good life in the past, but I simply wasn't aware of it. I am grateful for the awareness I got.

Enjoy your good health while you have it! Also enjoy small things, such as time with your family.

Things are also possible without a deadline, time or a calendar.

'Our greatest glory is not in never falling, but in getting up every time we do.'

– Confucius –

Take small steps

Start close by. If you've got a large project in mind, it helps to know that you don't have to do everything at once. In fact, most people hold back their first step at the thought that they must first command a view of the whole.

When I set up Coins for Care, I fortunately had no idea what kind of enormous project I was bringing onto myself, otherwise I would have never started it. And just because I made the first step, and then the second, and the third, at some point I was in the middle of it and I became confident that I would also be able to take the next steps.

'How do you eat an elephant? Bit by bit…'

When you step out of your comfort zone for the first time, start with a small step just so you can experience what it feels like and how you will react. If all goes well, you can begin taking more or slightly bigger steps.

If you want to set up your own business, don't immediately give up your current job. Start with the first steps in your spare time (a business plan, website, business cards, networking, first projects or clients). As soon as it catches on, you can consider working a day a week less on your paid job and spend that extra day on your own business. When you start generating sufficient income and feel confident enough, you can slowly transition to being self-employed. Should you choose to begin your business directly, you could follow the example of Hilda and Bas (page 46) and take on freelance assignments in order to generate some temporary income.

If you want to emigrate, first spend a few vacations in the country you want to live. If you enjoy it, do a house-swap for some months before burning all your bridges.

After one of my speeches, a young woman in the audience told me that she wanted to turn around her life after having traveled in Australia for six weeks. She didn't want her work in the turbulent financial industry to drive her crazy, as it was keeping her busy day and night. Instead of giving up her job (as she did enjoy the work in itself), she found a less radical solution. Directly upon returning home she bought an extra phone, which she only used privately. She would turn off her work phone after hours and in weekends. She also stopped checking her business emails outside office hours. 'These small adjustments give me an enormous amount of freedom,' she explained. 'I used to think that I should always reply to emails immediately; now I notice that people are also quite happy when I answer my emails the next morning.' Because of this relatively small step, she achieved enormous results and she can now peacefully think about a possible next step.

Adriaan (page 84) shares how he wanted to become an astronaut, already as a child. He knew this profession was only for a very select few people. However, he approached it very structurally and saw it as a long-term project. He read books about it, subscribed to a popular scientific magazine and saved up for a telescope. Now, as a student, he set up the foundation givemeaspaceflight.com to make a trip into space available to him and other students.

Initially, Hilda and Bas thoroughly dreaded having to organize their sailing trip and letting go of their pleasant little lives. As soon as they began with some hypothetical preparations, however, they got so much energy from it. Eventually they started looking forward to the trip so much, that they decided to do it. 'Without our step-by-step plan, it would have never happened,' they admitted. 'Only after you chop such a project into bits and list the action points, it suddenly becomes very manageable.'

Do you want to start your own business, but are you waiting for your first assignment? Seek out the places where you have added value to others and start doing it! Think about working as a volunteer or based on the 'pay what you want' principle. You offer to help your clients and let them decide afterwards what they believe your services were worth. This gives you the necessary experience, you make people happy and ultimately, if you really have something to offer, you will be rewarded. 'Pay what you want' takes away a number of obstacles and it gives you the chance to 'try it out' a few times before you start working 'for real'. Maybe you enjoy this method so well that you'll continue working like this. You can find a lot of information on this online.

With small steps you can often achieve more than with a big bang.
Mumbai is the most densely populated city in India. Instead of having lunch at home or in a restaurant, people got into the habit of having homemade, warm lunches delivered to their offices. Can you imagine: two hundred thousand warm meals that have to be delivered each day to the right person, exactly on time? And the next day the empty box has to be returned to the right house.
The dabbawallas, as the delivery persons are called, have developed an ingenious system. Forbes Magazine studied it and called it the most reliable supply chain in the world! Things go wrong only one in six million times. It seems incredible, especially if you consider that no computers are used and costs are extremely low. Moreover, the vast majority of the dabbawallas is illiterate! They use a coding system of colors and symbols to know where each lunchbox should go. There is no formal hierarchy or official organization. It simply works and it has done so for over 130 years already...

If you would try to set up such an organization today, it wouldn't work, not even if you would have all modern, advanced systems and techniques at your disposal. Consider businesses such as Fed-ex and

DHL. Their costs are much higher than those of the system in India, and they also make more mistakes.

What is the dabbawallas' secret? The system grew organically. In 1880 a few dabbawallas began delivering lunchboxes to English colonials who preferred eating their own food instead of Indian dishes. In 1890 about a hundred people were working in the system. It expanded in small steps until today there are an estimated five thousand dabbawallas.

Therefore, approach your dream with small steps. Imagine yourself as a sports star, with the ultimate goal of winning an Olympic medal. If they would put you in the stadium now, you would not achieve the results that are within reach if you prepare well. Begin with a training program. With practice matches, rest periods, good nutrition, training, fitness and coaching. Be aware that every step, however small, will bring you closer to your goals and dreams.

**Don't let life discourage you;
Everyone who got where he is
had to begin where he was.**

– Author Richard L. Evans –

Student Adriaan (23) wants to make a journey into space. As a student he set up the foundation givemeaspaceflight.com.

My dream is to make a trip through space. Unfortunately as a student and I didn't have the required two hundred thousand dollars. Therefore I was looking for sponsors to make me the first sponsored astronaut in the world. I even set up the foundation givemeaspaceflight.com specifically for this purpose. I want to show that space flight is not only for intelligent physicists, F-16 pilots and the extravagantly rich; it is for everyone. I also want to demonstrate that dreams can become real, even if they reach beyond the limit of the sky.

As a little boy I read about the space travels of Donald Duck and Tintin. Later I started reading popular scientific magazines and I devoured books by Jules Verne. I saved money for a small telescope and watched the moon from the roof of our house.

I always wanted to be an adventurer and I try hard to live my dream; not only in space, but also here on Earth. I long to go into space, not because I don't like it down here; I want to go because it seems like such a fantastic experience. I also believe that you must continue developing yourself as a human being; stagnation is degeneration.

My life as a student in industrial engineering was quite chaotic. I did some serious sports (rowing), set up an athletic league, earned money in all sorts of ways, naturally partied a lot and made some time to travel the world (I made a great trip to China). I was more successful in some things than in others, but I all the more believe that you should just do things!

I learned more from my givemeaspaceflight.com initiative than from my studies. I met many people in commercial space travel and I noticed that you sometimes have to be bold in order get things done; another time it's actually better to be diplomatic. I've had a lot of media attention in my home country, the Netherlands. I have been on national TV and radio programs, newspapers and even in Donald Duck magazine! Several motivators and entrepreneurs have shared my idea in their speeches. I am even going to be mentioned in a book about commercial space travel.

Therefore many people know what my dream is. Recently I was talking to a stranger in a small pub in Amsterdam. When I told him about my dream, he said, 'ah, you are that student! I already heard about you; I think it's truly great what you're doing!' So my dream is spreading and who knows, some entrepreneur or businessperson might read about me, and make that crucial sponsor that will make my dream come true.

The biggest obstacle for me is dealing with skeptics who find my dream nonsense. I always ask for feedback, because I noticed that you can learn a lot from constructive criticism. However, when I ask such negative people for suggestions on making my space travel dream come true, they have nothing to say. I have learned to deal

with my conversations with skeptics by thinking about people who DO believe in my idea.

It is sometimes uncomfortable when people ask 'and? Did you do it already?', to which I unfortunately have to respond with a 'no, not yet'. I was afraid that people would lose their faith in me. This is why I now focus on the things I did achieve. For example, I won a business-pitch competition. I am also now somewhat 'known' in the commercial space travel scene. This led to my involvement with ISTAspace, a startup in this industry. Richard Branson even visited the project! I also got to know important people who deal with space travel. ESA invited me to the opening of a new space center, for example, where, amongst other people, a minister of the Dutch government was present.

Because of these issues I started looking into how long it took before successful people eventually managed to realize their dreams. For example, the author of the Harry Potter books had been rejected by publisher after publisher; she persevered until, finally, someone said yes. Now she is world-famous and other publishers are probably banging their heads against walls about having sent her off. Here I'd like to point out Spyker's motto: 'Nulla tenaci invia est via', freely translated as, 'no road is impassable for he who perseveres'.

The best moments were those in which I was truly nervous. For example, for a special – five minute – news item on national television. The media can make you or break you for the general public, so that's quite exciting. When it became apparent that the item had turned out very positive, it felt extra good. At such moments I simply

know that at some time in the future my dream will come true. I then feel myself float a little, as though I am already in space!

I have just graduated from business school and will be a fulltime entrepreneur now. With a bit of luck I'll be able to buy my own ticket somewhere in 2020, and if not, I'll manage it by 2040. Come what may, somewhere in the future I'll be out in space!

If I succeed in making a trip into space in the short term, I would like to continue by offering other students the chance to also make such a trip into space. I want to set up a competition among students in order to stimulate entrepreneurship and a 'just do it' mentality. One of my main goals would be to spread a sense of corporate social responsibility and stimulate the realization of dreams.

My next short-term project is to run the northpole marathon in 2014. People will respect the physical challenge and I don't have to raise as much money as for the space-flight itself. Step by step I'll get to my goal!

Tips from Adriaan:

Everyone has dreams and ideas; the question is what you do with them. The Chinese say, 'a journey of a thousand miles begins with a single step'. My advice is not to think too much about the obstacles on the way to your dream, but simply to start moving, to act, because otherwise you'll never dare to take that first step.

And if you get lost along the way, remember that many roads lead to Rome. If you bear your destination in mind, you'll get there. Maybe the detour will give you loads of wisdom that you would not have had if you had headed straight for your goal.

www.givemeaspaceflight.com

**It's not who you are underneath.
It's what you do that defines you.**

– Batman Begins, 2005 –

You can have anything you
want in this life, by helping
others get what they want.

Networking

Contrary to popular belief, networking is not dishing out business cards and/or trying to sell a product or service. But what is it, then? The best description I found states that it is:

'...the bringing together of like-minded energy concerning an ambition or theme, including contacts and relations between any persons and/or organizations involved. A network seems to be organized in a noncommittal way, but it works compelling according to the principle of "taking and giving", mutual dependencies and/or agreements.'

So, you have a dream. You can't realize it on your own. What's more, you don't even WANT to do it alone! Therefore, share your dream with the people around you in an early stage. Practice your elevator pitch so you can tell your story in one minute, clear and convincing. Then ask everyone you meet for help and advice. Never again have lunch by yourself! And don't forget to give something back by helping others. Maintain your network; treat it with care. It is your social capital.

Networking is the most important thing you can do in order to bring your idea or project to life.

This part consists of the following chapters and interviews:

Share your dream with the people around you
Practice your elevator pitch
Ask for help
Never again have lunch by yourself!
Interview with Martijn
Help others
Interview with 'Auntie Leen'

Share your dream with the people around you

We often hear, 'I can't follow my dream, because my family, partner or boss won't agree to it.' This assumption may prove to be completely false.

Even in the earliest stages of your idea it is important to speak about it with others. This is the first step in the direction of your dream. Often it seems that partners, bosses or others whom you think of as a limitation, actually have incredible ideas for supporting you or maybe even want to join in themselves!

After a lot of pondering, Lucas Schröder decided to give up his job at T-Mobile because he wanted to spend a year sailing. It was his dream to participate in the difficult Ocean Challenge competition. Instead of accepting his resignation, his boss made an incredible offer: 'We'd like to see you back after your year off. Better yet,' he added, 'you'll continue receiving your salary and T-Mobile would love to be your sponsor.' To his surprise, Lucas had killed two birds with one stone: he could make his dream come true while keeping his job and receiving support from his employer. In exchange, T-Mobile had a great PR moment and a super-motivated employee. A win-win situation. Thankfully, these things happen more often.

Steffen Morrison was a team coach at the Dutch employment website Monsterboard.nl. He was quite content. However, a career in music was his big dream. During a yearly international business meeting, Steffen performed and won the talent competition. His Dutch colleague, Bas Silos, was in the audience. The two knew each other from work, of course, but they had never exchanged a word about their mutual passion for music. Bas is a songwriter in his spare time, and he had never actively searched for a singer for his songs. Carefully, Bas asked if Steffen would be interested in hearing his repertoire. Steffen was instantly enthused, and thus they began their collaboration. Monsterboard was also enthusiastic and gave Steffen space to work on his musical career during working hours, and actually perform live. This way, Steffen was able to unfold his talents and Monsterboard could show that dream jobs really do exist. Steffen received a firm basis for his musical career and Monsterboard was able to enjoy his qualities as a team coach a little longer. When his work became redundant, Steffen decided to devote himself entirely to his dream to be a singer. Meanwhile, he released his first album.

www.steffenmorrison.com

Hilda (see page 46) played with the idea of getting away for a prolonged period of time. She thought especially of traveling and sun. When she talked this over with her husband, Bas, he told her his dream was also to travel, but then by sailing boat! This was how their idea of a sailing trip slowly came into being.

Where Hilda initially saw drawbacks (dangers on the water, especially in combination with their small children), as she thought about it she also began to see great advantages (for example, it is great for the children to always have your house with you). They agreed that at each harbor they would be free to decide to continue their travels in a different way or to return home. This gave Hilda the peace of mind to gauge per trip if she was still OK with it.

When Hilda and Bas shared their plans with family and friends, they were initially rather critical about the journey where it concerned the safety of the children. However, later they even offered to join in on parts of the trip! This way, long crossings and multi-day trips were always made with three adults, which is much safer. 'Especially our various guests made the journey extra special, and in hindsight our friendships have been strengthened because we have traveled together,' Hilda explained. None of this would have happened if she would not have told her dream to her husband first and then to their family and friends.

One of the participants of my 'webinar' (a seminar on the internet) about turning your dreams into reality asked me what *my* dream is. I had never actually expressed it before, but I confessed that I would love to be a guest at the Oprah Winfrey Show, so I would get the chance to inspire millions of people. The remaining 50 participants of the webinar immediately began giving tips, which instantly brought my vague wish to life.

One of the tips was that I should publish my wish on the internet, so I will be visible to Oprah and the people around her. The next day I improvised a website: www.whyIshouldbeonoprah.com. Ever since, I frequently receive tips about Oprah from complete strangers. Unfortunately at some point I heard that soon she would stop with her shows, so I would have to act fast. Another person told me that she had set up a kind of competition for finding a talk-show host for her own network (unfortunately the audition is only open for American citizens, which I am not).

One of these people gave me a link to the National Publicity Summit: a very commercial event in the US, where you can speed-date with hundreds of journalists. For the astronomical amount of money you'll pay for it, you will be well-supported in fine-tuning your pitch. I thought: if I want people in the US to know that I exist and what I can offer, I will have to show it, of course. I decided to risk the step. In April 2010 I traveled to New York for the event.

This way I got around to practicing my story, I met many journalists, did a number of radio interviews and made contact with a publisher who is interested in publishing my book *What is Your Excuse?*

From experience I know that I'll still have to drink many more cups of coffee with many more people before anything will truly get moving, but at least I started something, and all simply by expressing my wish.

Practice your elevator pitch

Think up a good, short, captivating summary of your story.

Imagine. You're standing in an elevator, the doors close, and who is suddenly standing next to you? Exactly that person you were dying to meet! Whether it is a politician, the director of that one business you're interested in, a wealthy investor or whomever; this person can help you realize your dream! Now it's up to you to share your story in a single minute, in such a way that when the elevator doors open, this person will stick around long enough to ask for your business card. Many people and even businesses think they can already tell their story with conviction, short and powerful, but when it comes down to it, it still lacks something.

When I set up Coins for Care, I tried in vain for a year and a half to affiliate with charity organizations, shops, sponsors and banks. While at that moment I was fed up with constantly running into walls, I afterwards realized that in this period I practiced and fine-tuned my story an infinite number of times. This later turned out to be my big advantage. When, in a manner of speaking, the door was being thrown shut in my face, I would still manage to bring across the essence of my project in but a few sentences. More and more frequently the door would be kept ajar for me. Finally I managed to find the partners I was looking for.

Another advantage was that during the media appearances that followed, my elevator pitch turned out to be invaluable. On television you rarely get more than two minutes and a half. Fortunately I had learned to speak in ready-to-go sound bites and tell my story in a few short sentences. I also often already knew what kinds of questions would follow, and I would have my answers well-prepared.

Strangely enough, when I was in New York for a week to speed-date with journalists about my book What is Your Excuse?, it still took a number of days before I had found the perfect pitch for that project. You can tell from the reaction of people if your story has caught on. At first my story was too vague; they couldn't put it in a 'box'. The more I overwhelmed them with facts from my unusual life, the more I confused them. After a few dozens of conversations, one of the journalists said, *'so you are the "no excuses" lady from the Netherlands!'* and this stuck with me. When I opened all the conversations that followed with this sentence, journalists instantly knew what they were in for. This way they were able to ask questions that I would then answer with a part of my story.

In short: your elevator pitch is the most important thing you have, whatever you want to achieve! Whether you want to make a trip around the world, work less, help a charity organization or start your own business.

A good elevator pitch takes no more than sixty seconds and contains:
- who you are
- what you do
- why this is a good idea
- what distinguishes your idea or project from seemingly similar ones
- what you expect from your listener (be specific: do you want his contact details, sponsoring, a follow-up conversation, a reference?)

Please note:
Use words that rouse the interest of your listener, preferably in your first sentence already. My opening sentence containing *'the no excuses lady from the Netherlands,'* manages this: it makes people curious and they want to hear more.

On TED.com there is a video of a polar explorer who introduced himself in the following striking manner: *'My name is Ben Saunders*

and I specialize in dragging heavy objects around cold places...'
This one certainly sticks!

Ensure that your story doesn't become a memorized regurgitation; it should be personal and reverberate with your passion.

If a student applies to study Medicine and writes in his motivation letter, 'pick me, because I am so motivated,' then the letter could have come from thousands of other students. What makes you stand out from the crowd? Maybe as a child you were very sick and had to visit a lot of doctors, who finally cured you. Ever since, you have wanted to become just like them. This is a story that will stick. Please make sure that your pitch is unique; that nobody else can use the exact same story in order to appraise another project. For example, if you say, 'I want to collect money for a charity that helps children in Africa to go to school,' then it could be for Save the Children as well as for UNICEF and many other charity organizations. What makes your charity unique? Is it your approach? Or the country in which you work? Use this in your story.

Test your elevator pitch by exchanging the name of your business, idea or charity with another name. Is the story still valid? If so, you must further accentuate it until your name is irreplaceable.

Ben Saunders specializes in dragging heavy objects around cold places. See http://bit.ly/bensaun.

exercise

EXERCISE: practice your elevator pitch

First, write out your elevator pitch on paper.

Record your story on video or with a memo recorder and listen to it again.
Possibly exchange formal language with more colloquial language.
Practice as long as you have to until you're pleased with it.

Then, ask friends for feedback.

In the coming period, get in the habit of practicing your elevator pitch in all possible situations. Even if you have more time, for example during a lunch or at family gatherings, be sure to perfect your super short summary. If needs be you can announce: 'I am practicing the elevator pitch of my dream/project and I am very curious what you think of it. Will you let me try it out on you?'

Ask for help

Draw on people's qualities; ask them something that they'd love to answer 'yes' to.

Telling about your dream is one thing, asking for help is another step.

While practicing your elevator pitch you'll notice that everyone will automatically think along and give you tips.

People have a natural inclination to help. Most people prefer helping others over being helped. Why don't you create that opportunity for them?

For example, imagine you're a bookkeeper, and your neighbor asks for your help. Wouldn't you feel a little proud that, apparently, he has such confidence in you that he asks your advice? Make sure that you choose people who normally get less appreciation and address their specialism. Most people will gladly help.

And even the great people on this Earth can surprise us with their helpfulness. American Doug Barry experienced this to his amazement. Doug was fourteen years old when he decided he wanted to be a CEO in a big business. But how to go about it? he asked himself. He decided to go straight to the source and wrote letters to 150 CEOs of large American businesses such as Kodak, McDonald's, Intel, UPS and many others. Doug simply asked what the secret to their success was and what kinds of tips they could give him. Almost all of the business leaders wrote him back personally with tips and wise lessons from turning points in their lives! Doug bundled all the letters into a book: *Wisdom for a Young CEO*. It was such a success that he started a second project: he asked advice from famous people on how you can get the most out of your studies and he wrote a book about this, too: *Wisdom for a High School Grad*.
www.wisdombybarry.com

Networking is important in every stage. And this doesn't mean that you have to strew around business cards, but rather ask people to think along, be your sparring partner and refer you to other people who may be able to help. Don't expect results immediately. It is simply good to know and speak to many people, show them your added value and circulate your idea.

In his book *The Tipping Point*, Malcolm Gladwell explains that every social group knows people that he calls 'connectors'. These are the people who have many friends and acquaintances; a large network; a big social circle. These are the key figures that cause changes. If you're not one of these people yourself, you still probably know some. Make sure that you have access to many people and especially other connectors, via your own network or via theirs. Whom you know is sometimes more important than what your idea is.

It is common belief that famous people are unreachable. Did you know that they are sometimes simply in the phone book or that they can be found online, and that some of them may very well react to an email or a letter? If you don't try, you'll never know if it might have worked. Actually, why even ask a famous person? You can also ask someone in your own environment. There are so many lawyers, computer experts, accountants, marketing people and other specialists who'd be happy to think along; you only have to ask them.

In order to set up Coins for Care, I just called a notary from the phone book. When he heard I was setting up a foundation that aimed to help more than one hundred charity organizations, he was keen to legally set up the foundation for me. It took him half an hour and it saved me hundreds of euros.

What I learned from Coins for Care is not to put people on the spot. If you have a legal question, don't be too straightforward and ask a lawyer if he wants to help you with that issue. Instead, ask if you may show him something and if he can advise you on how you can best deal with it. Check if he knows someone who may be able to advise you. Nine out of ten times he will advise you himself, and in the tenth case he will probably refer you to a website or a colleague, who will, in turn, gladly help because you were referred by an acquaintance.

Never again have lunch by yourself!

If you really want to achieve something, then never again have lunch by yourself[1]. Invest this time in spreading your story and making or deepening contact. Find someone who is working on the same things as you – someone you (vaguely) know, a colleague, a neighbor, a distant cousin or someone you met at a party – and talk with this person for the duration of your lunch. Share what you're working on and ask questions about what drives this person. Automatically, connections will be made from this. Ask for advice, but don't expect more than that. Some things simply need time to mature.

Asking for advice sometimes brings about unexpected, surprising results. When Hilda and Bas (page 46) finally decided to make their sailing trip, they, of course, needed a boat. They asked advice from a friend who had made a similar trip with his family.

'He was one of the first people we told of our plan. It still felt a little uncomfortable sharing it so soon. We intended to sell our house so

---

[1] *Inspired by the cover of the book 'Never eat alone' by Keith Ferrazzi.*

we could buy a boat and we asked him for tips and tricks for purchasing one. Together we came to the conclusion that we needed a boat that was similar to the one that they had sailed with, which they still owned. Because his wife was pregnant, there wouldn't be much sailing in the coming year. This gave our friend the idea to rent his boat to us! This way, we didn't have to sell our house, which would make our return after the journey much more convenient. The boat was well-equipped for such a trip, which really made a difference. Together we also worked on the boat, before and after the trip, which was fun. Both parties were incredibly happy with this deal! Many people would find it scary to rent out their boat, or they might fear arguments or problems; we had therefore not once considered it as an option to borrow a boat.'

Because Hilda and Bas had asked their friend for advice, their problem was solved before they had even begun to see it as one.

How big is your network?

You don't have to know people well before you can ask them for help. Think of the hundreds of internet forums, for example for Mac (Apple) users. Users of these forums enjoy helping others. As soon as you ask a question, somewhere in the world someone will take the time and effort to answer and suggest a solution to your problem. The internet is a good place if you ever feel stuck with any kind of question. You can always find like-minded people who deal with any subject you can think of. Distance, time and even language are no longer a barrier.

While writing this book I used Twitter for posting the question: 'Who knows examples of famous people who first failed a number of times before they finally achieved success?' I was by the number of with reactions. Somehow, many people felt enticed to think along. They suggested scientists, sportsmen and actors that I would have never thought of myself. A number of these examples can be found throughout this book.

Connecting through social media such as Twitter, LinkedIn, Facebook and many other networks has the big advantage that people only react if they have time for it and if they feel like it. You don't have to feel guilty if you see a message come by and don't do anything with it. Therefore, make sure you're visible and easy to find via social media through social media, too, and that you tell your story there. It enlarges your network considerably. And the great thing is that people can find YOU, instead of you having to look yourself for potential partners, clients or like-minded people.

Laura Roeder is known as a young social media guru. She uses simple language and shows how you, as an entrepreneur, can use Twitter, Facebook, LinkedIn and so on. Most of her tips are freely accessible in the shape of short videos and her newsletter. For other information she asks a contribution. I have made extensive use of her vast archives with videos, tips and tricks.

www.lauraroeder.com

exercise

EXERCISE 1:

Map out your network. To which 'groups' do you belong? Where do you know people?

Make an overview. Think about, for instance:

- Work (your current job or projects and preceding organizations)
- School: elementary, middle and high school, university, or other courses you took
- Were you a member of any student unions?
- Sports clubs
- Other hobbies
- Family
- Through (the school of) your children, or (the work, the family or friends of) your partner
- Holiday/Travels
- Political party, labor union, charity organization, church
- Social media
- And so on

exercise

EXERCISE 2: a challenge

They say that it takes only six steps for anyone to reach the president within their networks. You know someone, who knows someone, who knows someone...and so on.

LinkedIn makes this visible by using a number to show how many steps you are removed from the person you are looking for.

Below are a number of challenges that can be solved through networking. Try to think how you might approach them.

? You want to meet the director of a large business that resonates with your dream. Maybe you'd like to work there, you'd like to offer your services as a freelancer, you are looking for sponsoring for your charity organization or you'd like to create a surprise for someone who works there. How would you go about getting an appointment with the director of that business?

? You need a live elephant for the promotion of...something. For your work, your own business, a charity, the birthday of a loved one; think of something. The question is: how will you make sure that there will be an elephant at the time and place you had in mind?

? You want a well-read newspaper to pay attention to your subject. Maybe you'd like to be interviewed; maybe you want to put a special person in the spotlight. At which section would this story fit best? How will you get in touch with the right journalist?

? You need a free airplane ticket to some destination. Maybe in order to hand out a prize; maybe for a charitable cause, a loved one or for yourself. How can you reach an airline that may be able to help you? Or maybe you know someone at a business that may want to sponsor the ticket?

© Petra van Vliet

Martijn (37) set up an outdoor business, lost a lot of money in bankruptcy, and built a megalithic tomb with fourteen thousand people. Now he uses his organizational talents to bring together people, ideas and information in order to solve small and large problems.

As a child I had all sorts of ideas, every day. I managed to make friends enthusiastic enough to actually implement these plans. But halfway into a project I would have thought up something new. My friends didn't like my short attention span.

Later I managed to turn this characteristic into something useful. I even made it into my job! I put things in motion and then find the right people who can continue the project.

My first conscious experience in this field stems from my high school period. I went from a school with two hundred students to a school with twelve hundred students. This was quite a shock. For example, the new school had a rule that students were not allowed to listen to their walkmans. The policy was so extreme that they would take away your walkman if they caught you. I thought this was ridiculous!

I thought: how can I change this rule? I decided to join the student board. I began collecting signatures. I made a list with all arguments in favor of walkmans (for example: you can disconnect from the outside world and therefore concentrate better on your homework). And I listed all counter-arguments, which I would refute one by one. After a while, 95 percent of the students had signed the petition. What was even more surprising, however, was that 80 percent of the teachers had also signed! I was only sixteen when I introduced the proposal to allow walkmans, accompanied by the impressive petition, to the student board. The proposal was accepted without any further questions.

I learned that you must have good arguments and bring them to light at the right places. Have a feel for timing and just do it.

What comes very natural to me is a barrier for many people. Others often think that starting something new is scary, or that you must have certain skills or resources. Many people tend to be afraid of failing, or simply have no idea how to take that first step. I discovered that 'untested assumptions' are often the problem.

The idea that something is impossible, improper or not allowed is so deeply engrained that many people don't even want to think about it anymore, let alone that they would dare to test such an assumption.

How can you test the assumption that something is impossible? There is only one way, and that is by simply trying it. Then you'll find out for yourself if it is possible, and if it is, how to go about it. Even if it does prove to be impossible, you will have learned something. At that point you can still decide to hold the assumption for real, or test it again at another moment, in another way.

If you're afraid of something, my advice would be to seek it out and see if it is logical to be afraid of it.

Years ago I started an outdoor sports business. I didn't have much experience in the field, but we were very successful. We had satisfied customers, fun employees and a good turnover. The business grew almost effortlessly. Everything we earned was immediately re-invested, so we did not have much cash flow. When a take-over kept being postponed we got into liquidity trouble. In order to save the jobs of my employees I had to sell the business at a loss. There I was: without a business, with a six digit debt.

I never faced a challenge as extreme as in that period. Do you know what I learned? When everything goes wrong, suddenly everything is possible: because it can't go any more wrong! You know you have nothing to lose. This is how I realized that if the worst thing you can think of actually happens, it isn't so bad after all.

Next, I wanted to build the biggest megalithic tomb in the world. By hand, just as humans did thousand of years ago. It is not known how they used to get this done, and nobody ever tried to repeat it. So that's what I wanted to do. I come from the Dutch village of Borger, where the biggest megalithic tomb in the world can be found. I liked the thought of letting summer tourists help along. Everyone whom I told about my dream loved it and wanted to help. This is how I started the project, and in the end fourteen thousand people played a role in it. Two years later we did actually achieve it: the largest megalithic tomb in the world, built by hand!

Those experiences made me realize that everything is possible, as long as you manage to bring together the right people, information and ideas. With access to the internet and social networks, this is now easier than ever before.

I see so many things that can be done differently and better; I have decided to dedicate my knowledge, experience, network, and sense of timing to solve small and big problems and realize opportunities. Among others, I advise the Dutch government on how to share knowledge internally and how to divulge information to the outside world. Young policy officers may know everything about Twitter and social media, but they don't get the chance to spread this within the organization. A lot of money is being spent on expensive consultants, instead of offering these young, eager employees a platform. Internet can also be used to get more involvement from residents and to make real use of the knowledge and expertise that is already present. It is a completely different way of working, and I really believe this is the future.

I love taking on challenges, so I enjoy working on today's more sizeable issues. I want to help set up enabling infrastructures and I want to do this together with awesome people. Themes that keep returning here are food, poverty, conflict, money, sustainability and so on.

I carry out my mission, knowledge, experience and ideas in different ways and I try to connect people in my network with each other.
I do this by:

- Giving key-notes and presentations: I give more than a hundred talks per year and I get way more invitations than my calendar can take. I therefore choose the places where I can have the biggest impact or reach the right people. I also make sure that there are video recordings of most presentations available on the internet.
- Stand-up Inspiration: We hand the microphone to extraordinary people so they can share their inspiring ideas. These presentations are also filmed and the videos are put online. See www.standupinspiration.com/about/.
- Being a lifehacker.com. Our Dutch platform gives practical tips to people and organizations for designing their lives in a smarter way. Lifehacking is the unconventional use of IT and other simple tools to help you cope with information overload.
- participation in various 'think tanks'.
- I promote the availability of interesting books on the internet, so this knowledge becomes freely accessible for everybody.
- 7 days of inspiration: inspired by the clean-up campaign in Estonia (where fifty thousand people cleaned up the whole country in a single day, see page 37), we wanted to make the Netherlands a little better, without spending any money. Our problem was not a pile of rusty refrigerators in the forest, however, but the fragmentation of ideas, organizations and people. From February 28th to March 4th 2011, the whole country was upgraded in seven days. Each day we took one subject and we brought together ideas, innovations, knowledge, people and organizations in this field. On Monday we upgraded education, on Tuesday we upgraded healthcare, and so on. The last day there was a big party in order to celebrate that we made it. We believe you can create value by connecting as many people and means differently and by developing new forms of collaboration. This will result in the best ideas and decisions.

Pay what you want

So I am constantly busy meeting, inspiring and connecting people. I travel all over the country and I spend about one day per week in my house in the north of Holland. I do this work because I think it's important to spread the good ideas I come across. Sometimes I am paid for this, but I certainly don't do it for the money.

I work according to the principle of 'pay as you want', which, by the way, is not a synonym for 'free'. My client decides what my contribution was worth, and afterwards transfers me some money. Sometimes I get five hundred euros, sometimes I get five thousand, sometimes nothing. Frequently I experience that my ideas on valuation are so renewing that many people have trouble making a mental picture of it. What's more, some ideas on this undergo a paradigm shift.

A paradigm is a collection of rules (written or unwritten) that does two things: 1) it defines boundaries and makes them clear, and 2) it dictates how one should act within these boundaries in order to be successful.

A paradigm shift means: a change to another game with another collection of rules. By thinking that 'the world' is as we see it, we create a 'mental prison'. The bars of such a prison are the blockades in our thinking.

One way or another I can look over the old prison walls and see what the world outside of it could look like. I try to give people and organizations such as the government insights into new possibilities and I especially help them to identify chances. If you can take away the fear of the unknown, a whole new world with unprecedented possibilities lies open to us all.

www.martijnaslander.nl

© Punkmedia

Matijn's tips:

The first step is often something simple. For example, if you want to
contact a company, but you know nobody
who works there, you can use the following
'trick'. You call the reception desk and ask,
'who is the most fun person who works at
this company?' Next, after some laughter,
you'll get put through to someone and you
tell him or her: 'according to the reception-
ist, you are the most fun person who works
at this company!' You'll have his or her
undivided attention and genuine interest for
a moment, guaranteed. Spend the next two
minutes explaining your idea, or ask if you
can come over for a coffee sometime.

Dare to ask! If you don't ask for help, nobody
can think along with you.
Many people prefer helping over being helped.
Give them this opportunity. If you don't ask
them, it is a missed opportunity for yourself
and for them.

Do you want to learn out-of-the-box thinking?
Allow yourself to be inspired. This means reading a lot and meeting many people. Read weirdly
and wildly.

Learn to get things done without any money.
Often you can get a lot done with very little.

Test your assumptions and thoughts. The only way to do this is by discovering and doing.

Social capital is a lot more powerful than monetary capital (money). Your social capital consists of your:
- reputation (people prefer helping nice people)
- network (scale advantage)
- visibility (if you hide away, nothing will happen)
- ability to bring people together

Access (network) is worth more and gives more status than tangible possessions.

Every problem contains a gift. If you are miserable or in trouble, go look for that present. If you focus on that one positive aspect you will have a completely different perspective on things.

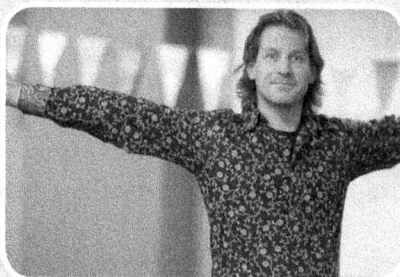

© Punkmedia

Help others

By giving, you focus on what you have to offer, which invites more abundance into your life.

An important aspect of networking is interaction. You give something and you receive something. Of course this does not always have to be from and to the same person or organization or at the same moment. You can receive something from one person and give back to another person. Or spend a period in your life only giving and another period mostly receiving. This exchange can consist of physical items, such as money or products, but also of attention, time, energy, advice, information, knowledge, ideas and so on.

When you are trying to achieve something or to realize your dream, there's a danger of being too focused on yourself. It sometimes helps to concentrate on something else. Not only is it good and useful to 'let things go' now and then; you may also get new inspiration. Meeting new people and especially helping others generates a lot of energy, of which both parties can benefit. And who knows, the other might do something for you in return, or for someone else. In conclusion, one of the most important tips in this book remains to talk about your dream with others. There are people who are looking exactly for what you have to say or what you might be able to do for them! Therefore, help others occasionally and don't expect anything in return. Do it from your heart. You might be surprised one day by something positive that comes your way.

I set up Coins for Care because I wanted to do something charitable. Next, my motivation became to fight injustice in the world of charity organizations. It cost me a lot of time, energy and money to keep this up for seven years. It was never my intention to improve my personal circumstances with this project, or to get something for it in return. Back then, it felt mostly like giving. In hindsight I did actually 'receive' a lot for it. I learned a humongous amount of things. I developed myself, met incredible people and I now have a huge network. And - I could not have imagined this beforehand — I am now frequently asked as a motivational speaker, partially thanks to Coins for Care. The fun thing is that by sharing my experiences, I now help and inspire other people and organizations.

Whether you are an accountant, an artist, a construction worker, a factory owner, a secretary, MD or a housewife; you have knowledge, experience and qualities with which you can help other people. Even if you can't think of your added value to others, time and attention for another person are often more valuable than you may realize.

Make a habit out of occasionally helping people. It can be something small: a compliment, a cup of coffee, a kind conversation. Maybe you can also help people with something bigger: by giving away something you no longer use (how full is your attic or basement?) or by offering your talents to help someone with a specialist service, filling in a tax declaration form, cleaning up someone's home or offering a ride.

Why would you do this?
- It may give you satisfaction.
- You will actually help another person.
- You can learn from the experience.
- You will become more visible and recognizable as an 'expert'.
- You will no longer have to wait for a (paid) assignment; you can get started immediately.
- It will provide social contacts.
- You will grow as an individual.
- Your network will extend; you will get to know new people.
- You hope that when you need it, someone else will be there to help you.

Next to money there are many other ways to express value. Information, knowledge, ideas, attention, compassion and access (to people, organizations, networks) are also expressions of value that can help fulfill your purpose on this planet. The great thing about knowledge, access and ideas is that you can give them away a limitless number of times, without having less of it yourself. You help someone, and at the same time you put them in a position where they are able to give something back to the world.

If you offer to help people in the field of your new business or dream, or with a talent that you want to develop, it can also become a part of your 'business plan' or plan of action. You practice, gain experience, get feedback, develop a customer database, and so on.

A few ideas:
- Make people happy with old things from your garage or attic (put it on eBay for free)
- Help strangers with all sorts of random things.
- Offer single moms on welfare a service or product for a fixed price
- Teach people about your hobby or expertise through internet forums
- Random acts of kindness – Oprah Winfrey

Pay It Forward is a drama film from 2000, based on the book of the same title by Catherine Ryan Hyde. In the movie (a personal favorite!), a social-studies teacher assigns his students to think of a project that will improve the world. He challenges them to really put their idea to action. Twelve-year-old Trevor thinks up "Pay it Forward". Trevor helps three people. When they ask what they can do in return, he asks them to help three other people instead. The idea is that these three people will, in turn, also do favors for three more people each, and so on. Initially the idea seems to have failed, but after a while it catches on; this causes incredible changes in Trevor's surroundings.

Pay It Forward is also an organization that exists in real life, founded by the writer of the book. More countries followed her example. See www.payitforwardfoundation.org.

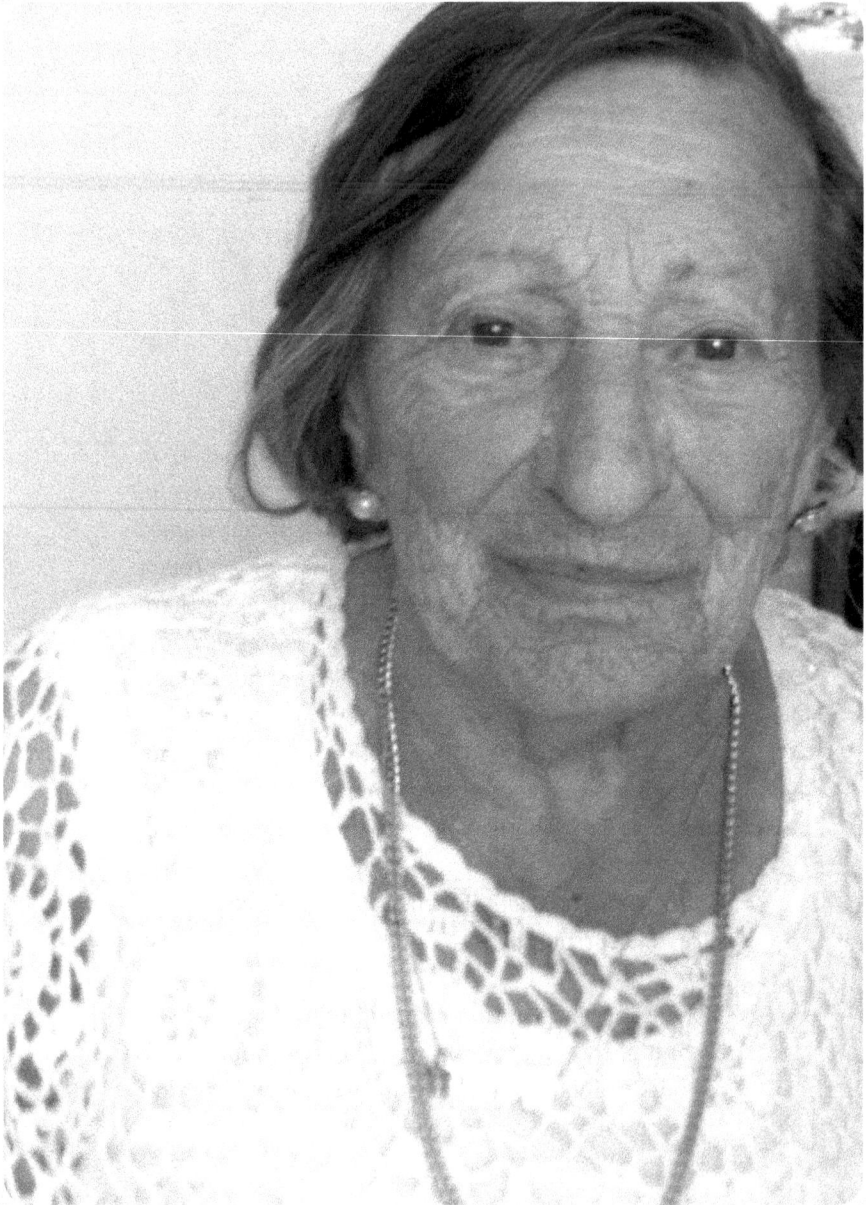

'Auntie Leen' (88) was the only one in her family who survived the holocaust and concentration camp Auschwitz. In spite of this, she continues to believe in mankind's inherent goodness. She now dedicates herself to countering discrimination in schools.

I have actually had a very protected childhood, in a straitlaced family. I was a little sickly and they called me 'the weakling of the family'. My mother always took care of me. I had a special bond with her. My father had a good job and we were rather privileged. Before the war I had already been to England and every other week we'd spend a weekend with family in Belgium.

When I was seventeen I became an apprentice shop assistant at a prestigious department store. I was very happy. I got engaged, I loved my parents and my little brother; I hardly ever thought about the future.

At the start of the Second World War, my parents did not tell us children anything. We had a radio at home, which was an exception in those times, but our parents shielded us from the news. We therefore had no idea what was going on. One day my father was fired from his job together with all the other chefs in his business, because they were Jewish. When I received a letter that I had to report myself for transport to Westerbork concentration camp, we went into hiding.

In the twenty-six months that followed we stayed in many different places. For safety reasons our family was split up. I only saw my parents and brother for a meager fourteen days in that period. And I never saw them again afterwards...

I was twenty when I was finally arrested by the Germans. It turns out I was betrayed by my own fiancé! In the train on the way to Wester-bork I had a chance to escape. But I didn't. Where would I go? I still hoped to see my family and especially my mother, if need be in the concentration camp.

Eventually I ended up in Auschwitz. It is beyond words what hap-pened there. It was an extermination camp where Jewish people were gassed and cremated ceaselessly. The ovens were ablaze day and night. I will never forget that smell.

We hardly got any food and we were clad in rags, also in winter. We were treated like animals and our lives were in constant danger.

I was selected for an experiment by the infamous Dr. Mengele. Apparently, the idea was to discover the quickest way of steri-lizing all Jews, but I didn't know this at the time. The only thing I knew was that he spread a purple salve on my belly button, which made it grow outward. One day he returned and cut off my belly button, just like that. It hurt a lot, but I held my head high and succeeded in not crying. The only thing I repeated over and over in my mind was: later I can tell my mother that I was brave and didn't cry.

When the war was almost over, the Germans quickly tried to gas all left-over Jews. Just before it was my turn, they suddenly decided to transfer us to a camp in Czechoslovakia. This is where we were officially freed. The wound on my stomach had become infected and I was more dead than alive. I spent weeks in hospitals.

When I was finally strong enough to return to the Netherlands, there was nothing there for me. No family, no friends, no house, no possessions. There were hardly any emergency measures for those who returned from concentration camps or came out of hiding. The general attitude was that we shouldn't exaggerate and simply 'get on with life'. Strangely enough, this is what I wanted. I wanted nothing more than to be 'normal' again and to lead a normal life.

I was in my early twenties; still very young. I lived in the streets of Amsterdam and sometimes stayed over with some acquaintances. One day I was at a party, and a friendly young man asked me if I wanted to dance. 'Sure,' I said, 'but then you'll have to accompany me home'. He did, and he continued doing this for forty-one years, until his death.

His name was Sven Boeken and he became my husband. We moved in with his sister and brother-in-law. Finally I had a place of my own; I hadn't felt so good and safe for a long time. At last, we found our own house and I bore a son. Unfortunately, Andre is our only child; Dr. Mengele's experiments had had a disastrous effect on my reproductive organs.

My husband had also been in a concentration camp, but we never talked about what had happened. We tried to build a life that was as normal as possible. For example, I still work three days a week in my son's fabric store. It gives me peace of mind and I get to meet nice people. If I had stayed at home, I would simply wither away.

When my husband died, years ago, I decided to tell my story, after all. I was asked by an acquainted teacher to relate about my war experiences at his school.

Two girls at the back of the classroom, wearing headscarves, were clearly from another culture. They looked like two timid little birds. At the end of my story I pointed at them. 'You two!' I began. They cowered in fear. Then I told them, 'in your homes things are just like they used to be in my family, when I was young.' The whole class looked confused. 'If a friend wanted to stay over for dinner, my mother would simply add a plate and say, "if there's not enough, we'll just have some extra bread". Your mothers are like that, too, aren't they?' The girls nodded and they began to beam. Later they came over to hug me; they were so happy that their classmates had now heard something positive about their culture.

Look around you; everywhere you see misery inflicted by one human being to another.

If a Muslim does something wrong, then suddenly all Muslims are bad. If a Jew does something wrong, then all Jews are bad. But if a Dutch person does something wrong, such as Joran van der Sloot who received a lot of international media attention for the Holloway and Flores Ramírez cases, people don't say, 'all the Dutch are bad.'

You should judge people according to their behavior; not their beliefs, their country or the group to which they belong. We can achieve so much more by being kind to one another.

If we would respect each other more, let each other be and wouldn't keep such a close eye on each other, there would be more peace and more happiness.

Therefore I now give lectures at high schools a few times per year. I think it is important that children know what has happened. I tell my own story, the way I experienced it personally. I want to get a message across. Also as a warning. This cannot happen again.

I want to encourage children to understand that not a single person can help: it how he is born, in which country, with which religion and which skin color. Today, still, you notice that people who are different are treated less kindly. What happened to me can happen to anyone.

'Can this happen again?' a schoolgirl asked me recently. 'My dear, you're wearing braces,' I answered, 'if someone with a weapon comes and says, "everyone with braces must leave the room at once," you will leave the room. And it can be much worse...'

I have seen where this narrow-mindedness can lead. Let's all make sure that it never happens again!

I sometimes wish that I had never been born. That way I wouldn't have had to experience all this suffering. But I have been born, and I am still here, so I might as well tell my story. If this helps me stir a few people and wake them up a little, then all of it won't have been in vain.

In loving memory of Auntie Leen, who passed away in 2012.

No problem can be solved

from the same level of

consciousness that created it.

– Albert Einstein –

Creativity

If you do what you have always done, you'll get the same results. If you want to achieve something new, different or special, you will have to use different methods than before.

Creativity means 'solving problems with creative solutions'. And also 'thinking of new working methods using your imagination'.

Thinking creatively does not only help you to find these methods and solutions, it also helps to make the best of every situation, regardless of the means you have at your disposal. It is about thinking in possibilities instead of limitations.

Count on having to do with what you have at this moment, and use it to the max. This way you're not dependent on others, circumstances or conditions and you can get started right away.

Figure out what makes you unique. Maybe a bad habit in one situation is an advantage in another situation. Put yourself in the right context in order to function optimally and excel.

This part consists of the following chapters and interviews:

Mind shift: do not think in limitations, think in possibilities! No excuses!
Interview with Eef
Use what you have
Interview with Anne-Lyne
Turn your weakness into your biggest strength
Interview with Maanwilla

Mind shift: focus on possibilities instead of limitations

Are you facing an 'insurmountable' problem? Think in reverse!

During business workshops, I sometimes invite the participants to brainstorm how their company could go bankrupt within a few weeks. Employees, tired of all the brainstorming about lowered budgets, raised targets and better service, often don't know what to do with this kind of assignment. After a few minutes someone carefully makes the first suggestion: 'stop picking up the phone!' Someone else follows hesitantly, 'be unkind to our customers?' and the next thing you know, they're unstoppable. This exercise doesn't only generate lots of fun and energy, but after an hour you'll find that the flip chart is covered with points that only need to be reversed in order to make the business successful. A true eye-opener!

If you do what you always did, you will get what you always got.

It really helps to look at your situation, problem or challenge from a completely different perspective. By viewing from a different angle you will also come to different solutions. This principle is frequently called out-of-the-box thinking. Often, normal in-the-box solutions (such as better listening to each other) also work very well; however, someone has to think of the idea at the right moment and apply it, too. Whatever you call it, it will always be refreshing to see a problem as a challenge and view it from different perspectives.

Everyone knows the discussion on the glass that is filled halfway with water. It is half full or half empty? A better question would be: 'where is the tap?'

Don't focus on what you <u>cannot</u> do; focus on what you <u>can</u> do. Has the bus left without you? Then take a train. Is the domain name you wanted to buy already taken? Then think of an even better name!

When I moved to Curaçao I tried to rent out my house in the Netherlands. Unfortunately I did not succeed and after a few months I decided to go back to the Netherlands. After all, the empty house only cost me money and it would seem wiser to spend my time earning this money.

Two days before my return I received a call from my realtor that the house was rented out. 'But... that's impossible, because I'm coming to the Netherlands!' I exclaimed, surprised. 'Well, the prospective tenant wants to move in tomorrow,' the realtor said. He added that I had to decide soon. I asked for half an hour to consider the matter. I was panicking. What should I do now? I couldn't be without a house in the Netherlands, could I?

I called a friend and told her about my dilemma. I will never forget her reaction. 'Isn't this what you always wanted?' I still did not get it, so she continued: 'no expenses, no obligations? This is your ticket to freedom!' I took a moment to let this news sink in.

This was a very different way of viewing my 'problem'. Now it had suddenly turned into an opportunity! By renting out my house, I was liberated from its monthly expenses and my worries how to finance it. So I called the realtor and gave him the green light to rent out the house. I would temporarily stay with friends, or if need be rent a cheap room, somewhere. In the end this would leave me with a bit of extra cash each month and it gave me the freedom I had always wanted! I am still thankful to my friend for her unconventional insight.

On YouTube there's a fun video about a so-called new sport: liquid mountaineering. It is actually a very smart viral commercial for a shoe-brand (more than nine million people have watched the video), but it has been made in such a way that it takes a moment before you actually realize what it is about. It becomes more and more absurd and in the end quite funny. These guys take the term 'thinking in possibilities' to new heights. Search for 'liquid mountaineering' on Google.

EXERCISE: how out-of-the-box is your thinking?

Finish the following series:

M T W T F . .

Check page 130 for the solution.

Now for a true story. In a small town there were three stores in the same street that sold exactly the same things: domestic appliances. Washing machines, coffee machines, televisions, and so on. There was quite a bit of competition and they kept a close watch on each other. Now imagine you're the owner of the middle store.

What does your day look like? What do you want to achieve? What is your biggest concern? What would you do to stay ahead of your competitors?

One morning you notice that your left neighbor has put a sign on his store that says 'the cheapest'. You spend the rest of the day breaking your neck over the question how you should react to this. The next morning your other neighbor has also installed a huge sign. This sign says: 'the best'. What kind of sign will you put up in order to distinguish your store from theirs?

Check the next page to see what the owner of the store in the middle did in reality. I won't need to explain creative thinking any more...

FUTURE EXERCISE:

Another way to transcend your limitations is to place yourself in the future and look back to see how you solved the problems. If you look back at what you have done, it always seems more logical.

Now imagine that you have reached a moment in time where you have realized your dream. You have achieved everything that you had in mind. Look at it well. What does it look like? And especially: how does your success feel?

Now read over the following questions at your leisure and take your time in visualizing each question and answering it. Note: you're still living in your own, successful future.

Solution to the riddle from page 128:
MTWTFSS (this is no convoluted mathematical
equation; they're simply the days of the week)

the cheapest | **Main entrance** | THE BEST

- How do you feel when you get up in the morning?
- How do you spend your time? Are you working? If so, what kind of work do you do?
- Pay attention to your environment; what does it look like?
- How do you deal with others and how do they deal with you? Does something strike you about this?
- What are the most important changes in your life?
- With what kind of feeling do you go to sleep at night?

The advantage of looking back from the future is knowing that whatever you want has already been achieved. Therefore, you can look back at how you managed to do this. You can see which obstacles you had to overcome and how you did this. As you already know that you succeeded in overcoming them. The question is not if you succeeded, the question is how you succeeded.

Look back at the present from the future. What problems did you come across and how did you solve them? What could you have done in order to avoid them?

Take any lessons learned back to the present moment. Don't forget how your successful future looks and feels. Take notes to help yourself remember.

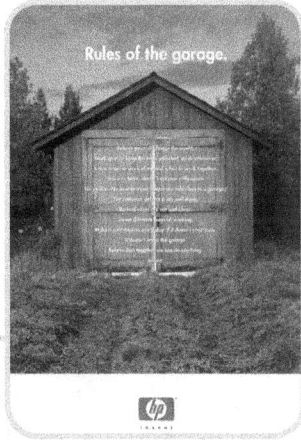

Rules of the garage

Believe you can change the world.

Work quickly, keep the tools unlocked, work whenever.

Know when to work alone and when to work together.

Share tools, ideas. Trust your colleagues.

No politics. No bureaucracy. (These are ridiculous in a garage.)

The customer defines a job well done.

Radical ideas are not bad ideas.

Invent different ways of working.

Make a contribution every day. If it doesn't contribute, it doesn't leave the garage.

Believe that together we can do anything.

Invent.

No excuses!

If you really want something, nothing and no one will stop you.

Some doubts and healthy nerves are normal when you start something new. However, don't let yourself be held back by a fear of the unknown. If you notice that you always search for excuses, focus your motivation in stead. Why did you want to do this, again? Try to visualize what your life will look like when you have reached your goal. How does it feel? What kind of influence does it have on your self-image, your relationships, your energy level? And now imagine what your life would look like if you don't take this step; if you simply continue what you are doing right now. How does that feel? How will you feel about yourself in a few years?

If you're convinced that this is really what you want, then pay attention to how you speak about the obstacles that you keep running into. Do you see them as a reason or an excuse not to follow your dream, or can you make an objective observation of the situation?
An excuse is frequently used as a reason to dodge a challenge. A factual observation, however, is the first step in the direction of a solution.
Use your creativity and imagination. Try to tackle your obstacles one by one with the help of this book and with the help of other people. Are you afraid of failure. See page 208. Can't do it alone? Involve your network!
As soon as you stop focusing on the reason why you can't do something, you can focus your energy on searching for a way in which you can.

Take the example of the American John Foppe, who was born without arms. He has learned to do everything with his feet, even frying an egg and drinking a cup of tea (see photo). In his book *What is Your Excuse* he describes how he learned to be creative with what was available to him, instead of focusing on what he could not do. 'Nothing is out of reach,' he explains with a healthy dose of humor. The principle that 'there is always a way' is a central theme in his internet video 'Armed with Hope'.

And it can always be more extreme. On YouTube you can find a number of touching videos by Nick Vujucic who has no arms and no legs! This inspiring man shows, with energy and humor, how he conquers obstacles in his life.

If these people don't use their situation as an excuse, then you can probably also think up a creative solution for your limitations.
Rainer (page 36) was not stopped by the excuse that what he wanted had never been done. Or that he had no experience, time or money. He wanted to clean up his country, Estonia, in a single day, and he managed to do this with fifty thousand volunteers. 'It is easier to get people in motion <u>for</u> something than <u>against</u> something,' he explains. Think about how much energy it costs to cling to your excuses and the status quo. Wouldn't it be much better to spend this energy on your dream? And on searching for solutions to challenges that you run into along the way?

On YouTube, Frenchman David Belle shows how he deals with physical obstacles on his path. His sport is called 'parkour' and David is one of the best! See http://bit.ly/davidparkour. (Don't try this at home!)

Chop your challenges into bite-size pieces

In my book *What is Your Excuse?* I describe how I divided the Coins for Care project into small steps so I would not be overwhelmed by the whole. If each step was doable in and of itself, then the total must be doable too, I reasoned.

I must confess something. While on the back of this book and in the introduction it says that I wrote it on a sailing boat in the Caribbean, it was there that I merely thought it up, in fact. I developed an idea of what it should look like, which people I wanted to interview, and what kind of tips I wanted to include in the book. But with all the beautiful islands that were begging to be explored, I did not actually have or take the time to work out the ideas. Afterwards, I was back home for a month and I did not manage to write the book, I did not do it, either.

When I returned to Curaçao I had exactly ten days to write my book! That sounded like a challenge... Still, one way or another I knew that I would manage. I had been in worse predicaments. On the other hand, as the deadline was approaching so fast, I did feel considerable pressure.

If I thought of the book as a whole, I did not see how I would manage. That's why I decided to look at each part separately; the chapters, the sections and the paragraphs.

I made a list of advice I wanted to give. These were the main subjects. For each subject I wrote a number of tips and examples I wanted to share. For each point I wrote a paragraph. Suddenly I would have finished a chapter; this gave me courage to continue. At a given moment I again looked at the whole and I could distinguish the five overarching themes, under which I would divide the tips. Most interviews also fitted perfectly with one of the themes. This made the whole even more coherent and valuable. By chopping the large challenge into small bits, it suddenly became achievable. And as you can see, I did succeed in the end!

Problems don't exist; only challenges

Success isn't a breeze. You often have to work hard for it. Problems aren't always a sign that things are not working out; they are challenges that you must overcome so you can soon enjoy your success all the more.

Inventor Thomas Edison once said, 'opportunity is missed by most people because it is dressed in overalls and looks like work.'

Don't let your chances slip away because life is not always easy. There is a tailor-made solution to every situation.

Imagine, for example, that you want to broaden your horizon. If you have to care for a sick family member, you can't go very far. But you can create time and space for yourself (think of the safety demonstration in the airplane on page 18. When cabin pressure drops, you must first put on your own oxygen mask before you can help others). When you have children that are of school age, you might feel restrained by compulsory education laws. Of course this has to be respected. But you can still spend school holidays in a different way. You can also temporarily live in a different country and let your children go to school there. You can also travel and homeschool your children. Or you can (say you will) emigrate and this way get out of compulsory education.

Are you in a wheelchair, are you disabled? You can do much more than you think. Take the example of Stephen Hawking. Hawking has a motor neurone disease, a condition that has progressed over the years and has left him almost completely paralyzed. He is also a theoretical physicist and cosmologist, whose scientific books and public appearances have made him an academic celebrity. Although himself English, Hawking was awarded the Presidential Medal of Freedom, the highest civilian award in the United States. There are many more people with severe limitations who have far exceeded our and their own expectations. With a positive attitude, a bit of creativity and flexibility you can achieve a lot within your capabilities.

Even if you have no idea where your 'travels' will lead you, do still take the first step. Experience has shown that the next step will become clear automatically; sometimes in a way that you never expected. When Daniëlle (page 26) took her broken heart to her father in Miami, she met the man of her dreams there! Eef (page 138) and Iko (page 202) changed their direction a number of times and they realize that after the first time, it gets much easier.

Richard Brandson says this is one of the secrets to his success: never saying 'no'.

Imagine no using the word 'no' for one whole day. In stead you see every suggestion as a chance. The option not to do it simply doesn't exist. Then you'll start thinking in chances and possibilities.

Jim Carrey made a great movie about this, called *Yes Man*. It's a real 'feel good' movie which gave me inspiration and left me feeling that everything is possible.

'Don't be pushed by your problems. Be led by your dreams.'

exercise

EXERCISE:

Choose a day (or will you dare to do this for longer?) when you may not say 'no', just like Jim Carrey. At the end of the experiment, answer these questions:

- How did this make me feel?
- What kinds of special things did I experience?
- What did this experience teach me that I can apply in daily life and in realizing my dream?

Watch the trailer at bit.ly/sayyesman

Eef (36) used to dream of a career within the family business. When it went bankrupt she made a definite choice for her second passion: photography. A few times she chose to leave everything behind and start afresh, for example on Curaçao. Her motto is: 'Just do it!'

I actually already had my dream job, as marketing manager at Ouwehand, the traditional family fishmonger business, one of the biggest brands in The Netherlands. However, a year after I got a new boss with whom I clashed immensely, I gave up my job with pain in my heart. When this boss left three weeks later, I felt I could not reverse my decision.

The motivation I needed to step out of the situation came in the form of an offer for a fun, international job. However, I did not accept it. Many people did not understand that I left my well-paid job 'just like that' and rejected the next job without knowing what I wanted next.

At some point I felt like I was my job. I was curious to find out what would be left of me when that part disappeared. I had saved some money and decided to live off of that in order to find out who I was without a job and what I wanted to do with my life. That's why I went sailing for a while in the South of France. Just to distance myself from everything.

I have always been very creative and did a lot of drawing and painting. My mother is an artist; from her I learned how to see, have a sense of color, atmosphere and composition. I was never much into photography; my sister was. When it comes to work and studies I opted more for the business direction. I did have an enormous fascination for brands, images and creation during my period as marketing manager. I was able to vent my creativity through new products, posters, flyers, a new company look, new packaging and all this well-tuned into each other. Sometimes I would even take the product pictures.

I think that I sometimes drove the advertising agency crazy, because I knew exactly what I wanted. I also wanted to learn to use the graphics program Photoshop, but I didn't' have time for it. When I left Ouwehand I suddenly did have time, so I started following all sorts of courses on graphics programs. Then a friend of mine asked if I would take pictures of her pregnant belly. She sent me a number of examples of what she was thinking of. This is how I ended up on the site of Tara Whitney, and suddenly I knew it: this is what I'll do! It simply happened. From one thing came another and I quickly had loads of great assignments.

During a vacation I fell in love with Bonaire, a tiny island in the Dutch Antilles. Still I thought the island was too small to live. I had, meanwhile, decided I wanted to live in the Caribbean for a while. I was flexible and unsettled: no husband, no kids, no permanent job; it was now or never! This is how I left for Curaçao, a slightly bigger island in the Dutch Antilles about which I had heard lots of good, although I had never been there.

I was unlucky. After the first month I got into a car crash and I spent the next month in bed with a whiplash.

Afterwards I went to work for an advertising agency to learn the ins and outs of the job. Photography was my evening-time work. This was so successful that I started doing it fulltime. I photographed for businesses and at weddings, amongst other things. By word of mouth I got more and more assignments. After working from home for a while, I was allowed to share an office with a business that I worked with frequently. This way I had colleagues while maintaining my freedom. It was a lot of fun!

When a wonderful year-and-a-half had passed I drew up a balance sheet. My business was successful! I would easily continue it. I had a super life on the island with many friends. Exactly at that moment my father asked me (finally!) if I wanted to be commercial director at Ouwehand. This was what I had always wanted. Even though the deal was not yet made, I decided to go back to the Netherlands. I knew that I would greatly miss my freedom, but the challenge made up for it.

Unfortunately one of the other directors at Ouwehand saw my possible arrival as a threat, which meant that my appointment kept being postponed.

In the meanwhile I was offered a nice job at HEMA, one of the Netherlands most famous department stores. Since my father's job offer I felt an itch to have a 'real' job. Because the situation at Ouwehand continued to stay so vague, I decided to work for HEMA.

After three days I already found out that this was not what I wanted. I think HEMA is a fantastic business, only the job turned out totally different than what I had been offered. Moreover, I remember that in an inspiring speech, the director shared that as a young boy he already dreamed of being the director of HEMA. Later, in the parking lot, I thought to myself: I'm living the wrong dream! My dream was not to work for HEMA. I had returned from Curaçao to work for Ouwehand, not for this. I decided to pick up photography. Surprisingly I again immediately got many assignments.

A few months later things were not going well at Ouwehand. The business was going to be taken-over, but this kept being postponed. My father asked if I wanted to put my photography *on hold* so I could advise the supervisory board. You don't say no to such a question. And so it was that I suddenly found myself in the middle of all sorts of negotiations with potential buyers, advisors and the bank, and I was the businesswoman again.

In the end the take-over did not take place, and after all sorts of discussions with other parties, the bank pulled the plug. After a fight that lasted four months, the business was bankrupt.

We were racing to start up again together with a holding company, so we could take over the business ourselves. This plan failed, too, and another business from our hometown bought Ouwehand. At moments like these, apparently it is the trustee in bankruptcy who has the final say.

It was a difficult time for the whole family. Apart from the emotional aspects, the bankruptcy also meant that the financial security that had always been there was suddenly gone. I dived into my work. Again I noticed that all sorts of photography assignments came my way the moment I was available again. I thought that I could just continue with my life, but then I got all sorts of ailments. Apparently there was still some grief in my body that needed to come out.

At some point I saw an advertising poster for Ouwehand, on which I, as 'model', took a bite from a herring. Seeing this suddenly made me cry my heart out. Everything came back at once. After one hundred and four years we had lost our family business. It felt as though a family member had died. Again, all the missed opportunities passed before me. This had been the third time in eight years when I thought I had the chance to return the family business to its full potential, but alas.

By letting the emotions out, I was able to close the book completely. Strangely enough, the end of this lifelong dream created room to devote myself entirely to my new dream: photography.

Photography is my passion; it really suits me well. I am in a flow when I take pictures. It gives me energy. This is an important measuring tool for me. I enjoy working with all sorts of different people, especially children. Creating something also appeals to me. To capture the essence of something gives me a lot of satisfaction. Business-wise it's going great. I've got a number of big clients and I can live off photography well. I have more ideas for the future. In cooperation with others I am now publishing photo albums and organizing an exhibition.

⊚ {www.eefphotography.com} ⊚

capture the essence!

Lately I have especially developed my creative side. The fun thing is that having your own business involves many businesslike things. I am now an entrepreneur, photographer, internet advisor and marketer, integrating both the creative side that I got from my mother as well as the professional side that I got from my father.

Strangely enough, Curaçao keeps pulling and I now go back and forth a lot between the Netherlands and that island. I thoroughly enjoy the freedom that this gives me. I know that if something doesn't appeal to me, I can always start afresh somewhere else!

www.eefphotography.com
www.divas-publishing.com

Tips from Eef:

Just do it. If something doesn't feel right, take action.

If you do what you love, it will come to you automatically. I can tell from experience.

Don't let financial security lead your decisions. This, too, can suddenly cease to exist.

Use your savings if need be (if you have any) to take a time-out in order to find out what you really want.

Your attitude is important. Believing in your dream is the first step on your way to realizing it.

Use what you have

Don't try to reinvent the wheel. Use what you already have and know. Don't wait for the perfect moment, that will never come: Start now! And, by the way, it's not about money...

Many people think that they first need a large sum of money in order to:
- start their business
- make a trip around the world
- work less
- and so on

Nothing is less true! It even stimulates your creativity to start with a small budget. An added benefit is that you don't have to postpone your project or dream; you can get started right away.

In *What is Your Excuse?* I describe how I learned to deal creatively with the circumstances and the means that I had at my disposal. At a given moment it even becomes a challenge to keep going, despite draw-backs. For example, during Coins for Care, I did not have the funds to produce four thousand collection boxes for foreign currencies that I had promised the stores involved. Normally these boxes would cost about $200 to $300 each and I just did not have that money, times 4000! Then someone came up with the idea to use sewage pipes! One yard long tubes were closed off at the bottom and at the top they were covered with a see-though cap with a hole in it, in which people could toss their coins. The tube would get a large sticker with 'advertising' for Coins for Care. Because the sewage pipes, stickers and production were sponsored, each collection box cost just a few dollars. I know for

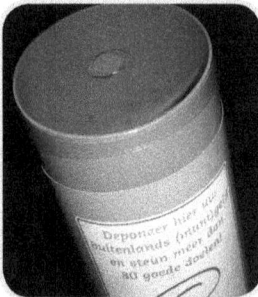

sure that the campaign would not have been so successful if I would have had a budget for the boxes, publicity and so on.

Have you got a steady job and do you want to become an entrepreneur? Just like pho-tographer Eef, you can start 'practicing' in the evening hours and on weekends. Slowly your customer base will grow, and at some point you can work less for your boss. This way the transition will be gradual. In the beginning, don't invest in storage, an office, your own production unit or other expensive items. Instead rent, lease or borrow, postpone large investments, search for a partner or think of another creative solution, until you have an idea of your income.

If you want to go on a trip around the world, then don't base the amount of money you'll need on your current spending patterns. If you now save in dollars and later spend it in rupees, pesos or another currency with an advantageous exchange rate, you'll need less money. Moreover, the cost of living in some parts of the world (such as South America, Africa and Asia) is much lower than in Western countries. Instead of saving more in order to cover your (relatively high) costs at home when you're abroad, I suggest eliminating these costs as much as you can. If possible, try renting out your house. Cancel subscriptions (this can be done before you leave already, to save money) and so on and so forth.
If you want to travel more cheaply, try a home-exchange or house-swap with someone in the country you want to visit. There are many exchange sites offering to connect people in different parts of the world.

Or check couchsurfing.org; someone might offer you a free spare bed, couch or other place to sleep. If you want a cultural exchange, become a member of servas.org. You'll stay over with locals for two days for free, and in this period, you'll exchange cultural and culinary information.
The following, somewhat older example from the business world that I have frequently heard shows how you can optimally make use of your circumstances. Dunkin' Donut shops were frequently troubled by armed robberies. However, extra security at all branches would be enormously expensive. Then someone got the ingenious idea to hand out free doughnuts and coffee to police officers in uniform. Ever since, the familiar sight of one or more police officers at Dunkin' Donuts has drastically reduced the number of robberies.

Fourteen-year-old African William Kamkwamba had to drop out of school for lack of money. Unable to read English, he browsed trough a book on windmills in the library. Following the pictures, he then proceeded to build a windmill, using garbage and other waste from his village. His windmill now powers the whole village! Watch the inspiring video on YouTube.

'Work with what you have'; can be taken quite literally. Lead by coaching agency magicoflife.nl, a group of parents of difficult teenagers asked their teens how they could best deal with them. They received surprisingly good and simple pieces of advice, from the experts themselves: their own children!

There's a funny YouTube video of a group of musicians (disguised as KGB agents) who break into the apartment of an old lady, and then start making music with everything they find there. And I mean literally everything: from her slippers to her toilet brush to the books in her bookcase. Search for *'one apartment, six drummers'* on YouTube.

Someone called Harrison Barnes posted a report of an event in the large lawyer's office where he used to work. One of the best female lawyers had a whole team of lawyers, researchers and secretaries working to prepare a certain lawsuit. Each day, her team was first in the office and worked on till late each evening and on weekends. The most expensive online databases were consulted; the best private detectives, advisors and experts were hired; nothing was spared to prepare this case meticulously. After months of hard work, Harrison heard the lawyer shout to her team, 'don't you realize that we lost the case to a guy who just finished his law degree, who has worked alone without any support, money or means, from a tiny office somewhere in an old mall?' An inexperienced lawyer who had but a fraction of their means had defeated them by making optimal use of what was available to him.

Twenty-one-year-old Alex Tew had been accepted into a prestigious English business university. But he was broke and scared that he would grow enormous study debts. Therefore, he needed money to pay his studies. The only thing he knew he was good at was thinking up ideas. Before going to sleep he would brainstorm: how do I earn one million dollars?

Next, he wrote down three conditions. The idea had to be simple to explain and easy to set up, generate lots of media attention and have a good name. Suddenly he knew it! He set up the website www. milliondollarhomepage.com and sold the one million pixels on the homepage for one dollar a piece.

It was the first advertizing website of its kind, set up by a student who used the proceeds to pay for his studies. This combination, together with the striking name, generated a lot of media attention and made the site into a success. In no time all pixels were sold and Alex had earned his first million. Alex made the most of his tricky situation, and meanwhile, his idea has frequently been copied.

Make smart use of the internet, social media and free publicity. You often have more than you think if you count your network. Internet is also a fantastic place to bring your initiative to life and for asking for help, knowledge and advice, and possibly for finding partners (see 'Networking', page 91).

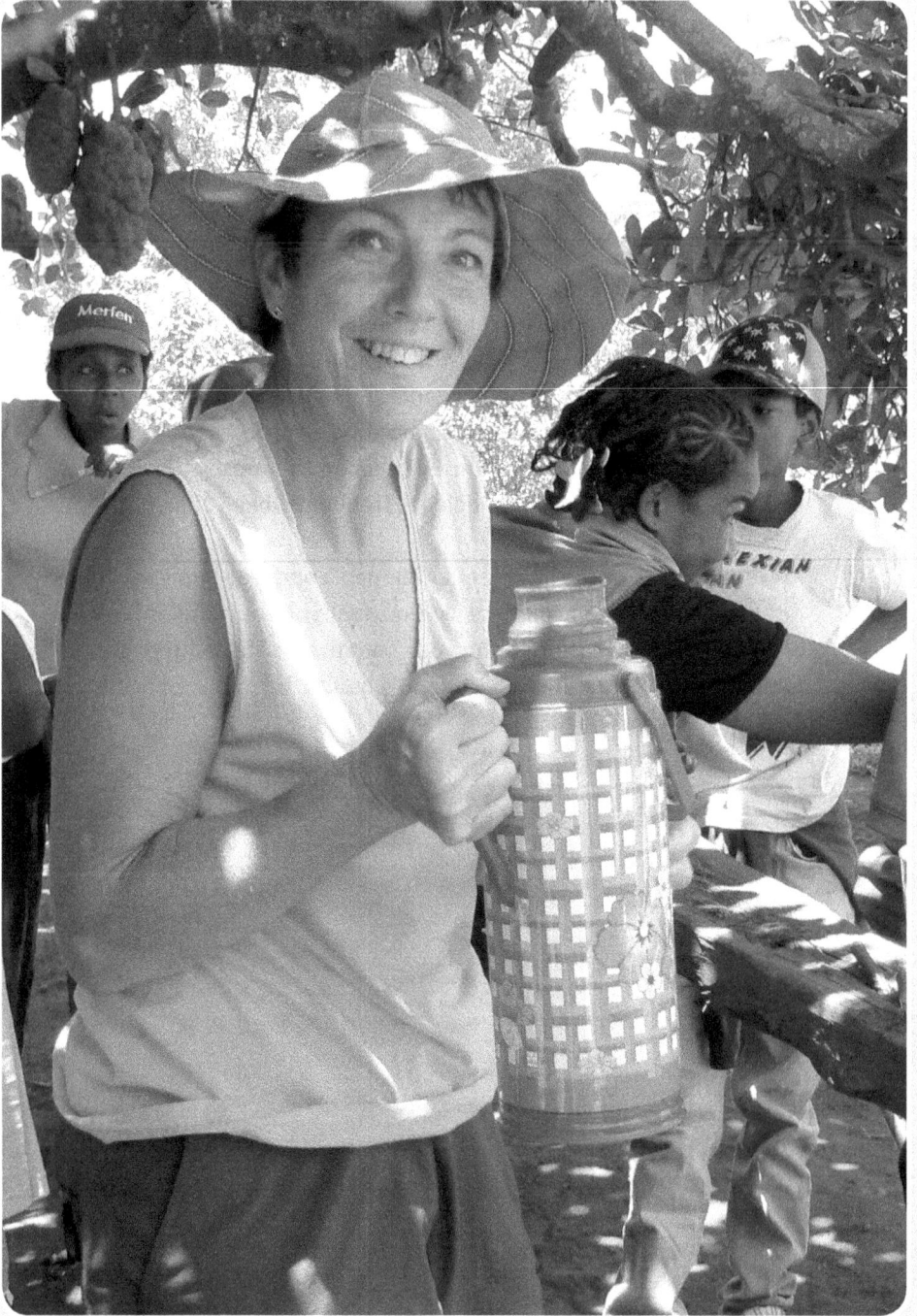

Anne-Lyne (56) is a teacher at an elementary school in Switzerland. Despite a serious illness, she worked as a volunteer in Madagascar for six months and fell in love with the country. Now she puts all her spare time and meager finances in small projects that she manages herself.

At a given moment I discovered that after working at a school for ten years, you earn the right to six months of paid leave. You can spend this time on a study, travelling or a hobby; a committee will judge if your suggestion develops your capacities as a teacher and sufficiently contributes to your personal development. I was surprised that almost nobody made use of this. My colleagues indicated that they wouldn't know what to do with their time off, or that they wouldn't be able to deal with the uncertainty...

I had been to Madagascar once with friends whose children had been born there. I instantly fell in love with the country. Nature is so beautiful; the people know a lot of misery but they are still so friendly. I call it 'le sourire dans la misère' (a smile within the misery). We came to a small village where an orphanage, a clinic and a school had already been set up. I decided that I wanted to spend my six months of leave there, as a volunteer.

But it almost did not go through. I became seriously ill and spent two years in and out of the hospital. I grieved over my project, but hardly had any energy and only barely succeeded in dealing with normal, daily problems.

One morning I woke up with a deep conviction; a voice that kept on saying, 'write your project plan, come on!' True, I thought, if this takes any longer, I'll be too old to go away for half a year. At the same time I became doubtful. I can't just go to a foreign country if I'm still so sick? And I'm actually already too old. I don't know what to write in my proposal... One excuse after the other came in. Still, I decided to write the project proposal. My friends helped me with this, because I wasn't able to think coherently. When I handed it in, I wasn't yet capable of acting it out, but I hoped and believed that I would get better.

One night I dreamed that I was healed. I couldn't believe it, at first. The doctors were skeptical, too, but from that day onward my energy slowly returned. This felt so good! Slowly I became the person I used to be. That dream was a breakthrough for me. That day I decided to go. I realized that there would always be a reason or an excuse not to do it, but if I would wait any longer, I knew I would never go to Madagascar. I would have to be careful with my health, but I had decided: I'll simply do it!

In 2007-2008 I returned to the projects that I had visited eight years before. This had to happen completely officially, through a special committee that thankfully accepted me. I began to give French lessons at the school there, and also handicrafts: children there are not stimulated in their creativity at all. Together with a female local doctor I also gave lessons in the basics of health and hygiene.

Moreover, I worked with women's groups to invite them to talk about their feelings, which is really not a habit in Madagascar. Saying 'no', for example, is not a part of their culture at all. It is special to see their developments: the first weekend nobody said a word; the second time they were a lot more open and dared to ask questions on sexuality and other personal subjects.

Ever since, I try to go back for two months each summer. I don't manage each year, but often, at the last moment, everything works out after all. The rest of the year I can still do loads from a distance.

Over the past years a school has been set up for children aged four to six. Previously there had been absolutely nothing for this age category. The tables and chairs were much too high for them; I had them made to size on the spot. It is important to share the project with the people themselves. Parents pay half of the costs: one dollar per month.

One thing led to another. I am now even involved in a number of agricultural projects, even though I know nothing on the subject! But I did find some people who do, and they are now showing the best way to grow crops in Madagascar.

My own money and the contributions of friends and family amount to a yearly sum of approximately a thousand dollars to spend on projects in Madagascar. This may not seem much, but we can do loads with it. Local people come with suggestions. This house needs to be repaired, that school needs help, and so on. Together we choose a number of projects and we make a budget. I get before and after pictures of all repair projects and an itemized bill. Everything is done by locals. It is incredible to see this change in mentality.

Ever since I've been coming to Madagascar, I've been living more and more in the now. I used to live for the future or think only of the past. My dream is to be able to enjoy the present moment even more.

Everyone is helping out....

I have learned that you're never too old to do something for others or start something new. It isn't your age that counts; it's your attitude. You must have faith and be strict on yourself. And I especially learned that you have to let go. There is always a solution.

Tip from Anne-Lyne:

Let go of your fears and do not get too attached to material things. Everything is so relative.

Think differently

Here's to the crazy ones. The misfits. The rebels. The trouble-makers. The round pegs in the square holes.

The ones who see things differently. They're not fond of rules. And they have no respect for the status quo. You can praise them, disagree with them, quote them, disbelieve them, glorify or vilify them.

About the only thing you can't do is ignore them. Because they change things. They invent. They imagine. They heal. They explore. They create. They inspire. They push the human race forward.

Maybe they have to be crazy.

How else can you stare at an empty canvas and see a work of art? Or sit in silence and hear a song that's never been written? Or gaze at a red planet and see a laboratory on wheels?

While some see them as the crazy ones, we see genius. Because the people who are crazy enough to think they can change the world, are the ones who do.

This was an advertising campaign for the brand Apple.

Online you can also find the stunning short video: http://bit.ly/thinksein.

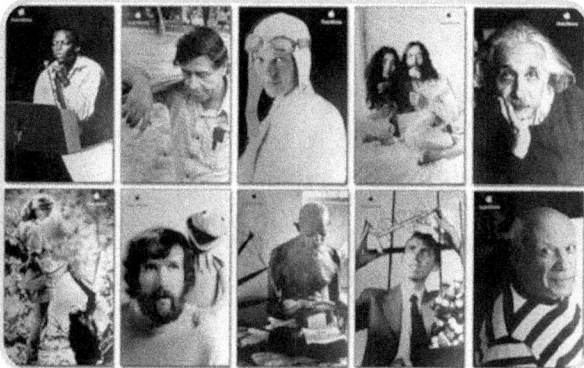

Turn your weakness into your biggest strength

All personal characteristics have two sides. In different circumstances the positive or the negative aspect of that same trait can be empathized. If you are very precise, for example, you will be much valued as an accountant or a bookkeeper, but in an entrepreneurial environment you may be branded as inflexible or a nitpicker. If you are someone who quickly takes initiatives, this will be seen as leadership in one situation and in other cases as authoritarian.

'I have no special talent, I am only passionately curious.'

– Albert Einstein –

Did you know that Oprah Winfrey was fired from her first job at Nashville TV? All because she constantly burst out in tears; this was how involved she was with the suffering of the main characters in her reports. As a newsreader, too, she appeared to be too emotionally involved with the coverage. Every so often her superiors would have to set her straight. In the end she did seem very suitable for a local talk show. The emotional approach to her subjects even drew the attention of famous television station ABC, and so it was that Oprah became the most famous talk show hostess in the world.

Martijn (page 106) explains that his short attention span used to be seen by friends as a handicap, but he now manages to use this characteristic for important innovations that stimulate our economy and our society.

I have experienced firsthand how you can create or seek out the right circumstances where your 'weaknesses' become your biggest strengths.

You see, many people used to think I was too 'pushy'. My friends and my colleagues all knew that once I had something in mind, or if I went for something, nothing could stop me. Sometimes my passion and enthusiasm were experienced as irritating by colleagues who were less than happy with a certain initiative.

When I set up Coins for Care and had to organize all sorts of things against the current and without a budget, this characteristic turned out to be invaluable. I did not accept 'no'; not from the banks who did not want to exchange foreign currency, not from sponsors who said, 'if I help one charity, all of them will soon want my help' (to which I answered: 'then you're in luck: Coins for Care helps over a hundred charities, so you'll be done in one go!'). I also did not accept 'no' from the established charity world, that said, 'just let us be, why change? Why make things cheaper and do things with more transparence? We've always done things our way, and aren't things going well enough like this?' In the normal world I was too pushy, and suddenly in the charity world I was a go-getter, admired for my persistence and enthusiasm.

I also got used to (and learned to work with) my girl-like looks. In some cases this is an advantage (people do not feel threatened by me); in other cases it is a disadvantage. When I wanted to set up Coins for Care, nobody took me seriously. I was a naïve, young, blonde girl, without a track record. I had no budget, no experience, no well-known name and no large organization backing me. Initially I did not find any partners; nobody dared to connect his name to such an indefinite initiative.

At some point, chance had it that I was invited for an interview on a national tv show. Suddenly it appeared that my girl-next-door image was actually an advantage. My innocent looks helped to sell my idea to collect foreign coins surrounding the introduction of the euro. 'You bring the idea very close to our viewers,' I was told on multiple occasions. 'You give them the idea they could have thought of it themselves.' If I had been a large, well-known organization, I would not have been able to get the same enormous amounts of free publicity as I got now.

Nowadays I give motivational speeches and workshops, and I still sometimes make use of (or abuse?) my innocent appearance. Business representatives who paid quite a bit for an 'expert' to come and talk about the financial crisis, leadership or cooperation, may feel quite uncomfortable when I step onto the stage uninhibitedly, casually dressed and my hair a big blonde mess. 'Hello everyone, my name is Esther, I just flew in from Curaçao and I know absolutely nothing about...' I begin, after which I name the subject for which I have been hired. The whole room will look at me, shocked. After I sufficiently succeed at bringing down the expectations of my presentation, I continue, 'but as an outsider I have seen a few remarkable things that I would like to share with you.' Then I show them videos, newspaper headlines, quotes and articles that caught my eye, after which usually an interesting discussion follows. I consciously make use of my 'blonde-girl image' in order to take my audience out of their comfort zone, which helps them to be more open to the unconventional insights that I, as an outsider, present. This way, my tips and ideas don't come as a threat. Effectively, I facilitate people's abilities to come to new insights themselves.

Striking examples of people who turned their weaknesses into their strengths can be found throughout the history of the world.

In only a few years, Nelson Mandela made the transition from being a political prisoner convicted for life to president of his beloved South Africa. Nothing had been in his favor: he was black, poor and born in the wrong era in the wrong country. Still, his imprisonment and his subsequent worldwide fame worked to his advantage. And not only to *his* advantage; he had become the symbol for a whole race.

Composer Beethoven became famous for his talents and symphonies, which were modern for their time. Less known,however, is the fact that at an early age Beethoven started to lose his hearing, and at the age of twenty-seven he was completely deaf. He confided to his friends how difficult this was for him, both professionally as well as socially. Among other things, he wrote to them that as a deaf musician he did not actually want to live anymore, but he felt obliged to so that the world could enjoy his compositions. At some moment he hardly even spoke anymore.

While deafness and music are actually incompatible, Beethoven continued. He wasn't able to perform live anymore, but he did continue to write complete symphonies. A symphony consists of multiple layers of music, written for various instruments. This is mastership even for musicians whose hearing is completely intact. It is impossible to imagine what could have gone on in the head of this man. Because of his limitations, he must have taken extra effort to concentrate on his musical talents. During the premiere of his ninth symphony, Beethoven did not even hear the thunderous applause of his audience. Someone had to turn him around to show him the audience's exultation. Realizing that his symphony was a great success, and reminded that he could not hear a thing, Beethoven burst out into tears.

On the 'What is your dream?' YouTube channel you can find a few videos of even more beautiful, surprising and inspiring examples:

Stephen Wiltshire is also called the *Human Camera*. He is autistic and has trouble expressing himself. He spoke his first words at the age of five. He started drawing in order to give expression to his feelings. His family discovered that he had an extraordinary visual memory and took him on challenging expeditions. For example, after a helicopter flight of only twenty minutes, he drew the complete city of Rome, including the correct number of windows in all major buildings. Stephen had never been to Rome before!

Bulgarian Valentina Hasan sings a song in English for *Music Idol*. Since she can't actually sing well and doesn't speak any English, this takes courage. Valentina's version of the refrain of Mariah Carey's 'Can't Live' sounds like 'Ken Lee'. However, Valentina maintains in front of the jury that the phonetic sounds she memorized are really English. Despite, or perhaps because of her 'handicap', this Bulgarian singer becomes famous. A rage has begun on the internet where people try to sing just like 'Valentina Hasan of Ken Lee!'

Kseniya Simonova, a young woman of twenty-four from Ukraine, thought she wasn't good at drawing. She tried pencils, paint and all sorts of paper and canvas, but it simply didn't work for her. By chance she found out that she can make really beautiful things out of sand. 'It simply happens,' Kseniya explains. With an unusual act, Kseniya participated in *Ukraine's Got Talent*. Her sand drawings on a lighted glass plate depict how difficult life was during the German occupation in the Second World War. Few people know that no less than eleven million people of the forty-two million inhabitants of Ukraine were murdered. The sand drawings brought the audience to tears. The jury, too, was impressed. Kseniya won the show and went home with the first prize of 125,000 American dollars. 'I can't think of a larger compliment,' this special talent said.

If you have the feeling that something is not meant for you or that you can't do a particular thing, remember these people and think of how you *can* make a difference. Don't try to be like everyone else. Distinguish yourself in the field in which you are special, where you have something to tell or where you can create something valuable.

If you can't recognize your weakness how can you recognize your strength?

exercise

EXERCISE:

Write down twenty-five things at which you are good. Yes, that is correct: twenty-five! Start with the 'normal' things: maybe you can cook well, or you are good at mental calculation. If you force yourself to write down twenty-five things, you will easily arrive at a number of things that are uniquely you.

Ask your family and good friends for help. What makes you special? For what kind of things do they turn to you? For what do they admire you?

What is your weak spot, which may very well be your unique, hidden talent?

In what kind of situations does this characteristic flourish most?
How would you be able to make optimal use of this?

'What comes out of you when you are squeezed is what is inside you.'

– Wayne Dyer –

© Ilse Lukken

Maanwilla (38) is a speech therapist, single mother of two who is clairaudient. When she first discovered that she could hear more than others, she simply preferred to be 'normal'. After her divorce she decided to choose to follow her passion and use *all* her talents. With ups and downs she started her own speech therapy practice. She also gives voice and presentation trainings to business people, politicians and academics.

It has only been a few years since I discovered that I have second hearing (clairaudience, as opposed to clairvoyance). It still feels strange to name it. In people's voices I hear all sorts of 'hidden' information. This can be in the form of emotions, tension, blockades or traumas from childhood, but it can also reveal someone's strength and passion.

'I…spy…with my little ear…'

I always thought that my speech therapy education tought me how to hear from people's intonation what bothered them or kept them busy. At some point I did an observation for a speech therapy colleague, and afterwards we talked through the cases together. It turned out that by listening carefully, I had found out all sorts of things about the home situations and experiences of clients that my colleague did not hear. I was surprised and asked my colleague, 'can't you tell from the tension in that man's voice that he's going through a divorce?' and 'can't you tell from the breathing of this woman that she had a traumatic experience at the age of four that still causes some of her muscles to tense up?' No, my colleague could not hear this…

As a teenager I was passionate about singing and theater. However much fun I had with it, unfortunately I had to admit that I wasn't good enough for conservatory. In any case, I wanted to do 'something with voices'. When one day I had a sore throat and ended up getting speech therapy, I decided I wanted to study this. As a speech therapist, you learn to help people with everything that has to do with their mouth, throat, voice and speech, where it concerns problems such as stuttering, but also problems with hearing, reading and writing and, for example, with swallowing. It is a very interesting, broad field, and we don't only work with problems; we also teach preventive measures and, for example, how to make better use of one's voice in the case of people who give frequent presentations or those who sing.

I became increasingly fascinated by voices and what I could hear from them, and I wanted to know everything about breathing, speech and whatever links the two. After my speech therapy studies I therefore continued taking all sorts of courses.

From the start it had been very normal that I instantly 'heard' what caused the speech problems that I came across. I can sometimes hear on the telephone if, for example, someone is very tall, or if they broke their ankle years ago. If I mention this, people usually react very surprised. If you have ever had a broken ankle, the feedback of your tone of voice through your body is very different than that of someone without a broken ankle. Speech is nothing but vibrations. If you're shorter than average or much taller, your voice resonates differently through your body. If you have heard this difference once, you'll never forget it.

I can't recall ever not having had this ability. It surprised me when I realized that not all my colleagues listened the way I do. Maybe I never wanted to acknowledge it, because deviant behavior in our society is sometimes seen as 'scary' or 'strange', and I really wanted to be normal. Until that decisive conversation with my colleague, I had always been able to explain my telling observations from my studies. Ever since, I had to admit to myself that I catch more information than others and I try to help people this way. Fortunately it is becoming more and more accepted that there are people who observe things that escape others completely.

Sometimes it is difficult that I am so sensitive. If I don't close myself off, I am overwhelmed by stimuli. On the other hand, my sixth sense does quickly give me a deep connection with most of my clients.

At a certain moment I wondered what you could to do with speech therapy for people without any medical problems. This gave me the idea to start giving voice and presentation trainings through my business voicepower.nl. These courses also prove that I know exactly where to find someone's strength and how they can use it to their advantage. For example, I can hear if someone doesn't dare to give himself fully through some insecurity or other. I can help this person to overcome this and use their voice completely in order to get to the core of their strength. In my experience it feels great if you learn to express your authenticity by using your voice.

I am very good one on one; whether it is with my neighbor or a state secretary. But my weakness is that I am not good at marketing myself. If I have to write a proposal or a text for my website and I'm sitting in front of an empty screen or a white sheet of paper, I completely freeze up. Then I call in the help of my friends. I have a lot of loving people around me who help me with all sorts of things; they are a great support to me.

Through a friend I came into contact with a number of well-known people from business and politics that I now coach. These people don't choose me because I have second hearing. On the contrary! If they would know this, they may not actually hire me; it sounds too airy-fairy. They work with me because I help them reach their inner strength. I only use my gift in combination with normal diagnostic techniques for quickly discovering the ways in which I can best help a person.

After my divorce three years ago, my whole life was turned upside down. Occasionally I was through with the world, but I had to go on. Friends helped me with their listening ears, doing odd jobs and my administration, and by occasionally shoving me in the right direction. I had never had anything to do with finances and now I suddenly had to fence for myself. How do I create a safe environment for my children? How do I create a financial buffer for less affluent times? How do I create a daily routine? Much had to be organized. I had to move houses twice in a single year and I started my own speech therapy practice.

I wanted to see if I would manage to survive when following my heart, when doing something for which I felt real passion. I wanted to set up my own speech therapy practice so I would do something that made me happy every day. Well-meaning friends and family advised me, with some concern: why don't you get a steady job? But I wanted to see if I could make my dream come true.

I had to figure out things that I had never thought about before. How do I contact insurances, which software will I use, what kinds of materials will I purchase first? An enormous administrative rigmarole came my way. I had trouble to continue believing that I had taken the right decision.

In the end I simply started calling insurances. Straightforwardly I would say, 'I am starting a speech therapy practice, I would like a contract with you, what should I do?' The first time I was so nervous that I thought they could hear my heart beating on the other end of the line. But it was actually very easy. Now I tackle everything step by step.

Looking back, I think I have grown a lot the past few years. Strangely enough, the divorce also gave me peace. I now feel much happier than I remember ever being. There are many things that I still can't do very well, but I try to enjoy the things I did achieve.

I have learned to accept that I have a special gift and, even though it is sometimes a bit troublesome, I try to use it as well as I can.
I finally know who I am and what I want, and I don't let anything daunt me so easily anymore. Whatever happens to me, I know I will always get up again.

www.voicepower.nl

'It is our choices

that show what we truly are

far more than our abilities.'

– J.K. Rowling –

(Author of the Harry Potter books)

Making choices

The choice is yours: passion or money? There are but twenty-four hours in a day. How will you use them? What do you spend your money on? Does it bring you closer to your dream? In every situation you can decide whether the glass if half full or half empty.

Did you know there is a realistic possibility that your attitude and visualizations actually influence the result? This could be both positively and negatively.

What will you choose? Will you choose security, or will you opt for learning opportunities that may lead to success? Will you let your fears hinder you or will you let possibilities lead the way?

This part consists of the following chapters and interviews:

Choose for passion
Interview with Huub
Choose consciously what you spend your time and money on
Interview with Michaelangelo
Think positively and visualize
Interview with Iko
Don't be afraid to fail

Choose for passion

According to many people I lead a dream life. For other people my life is a nightmare. I have traveled through more than one hundred countries, I am an independent entrepreneur, I live on a tropical island many months of the year, I have written a book and participated in *Survivor*. I don't have a fixed place to live or stay, no savings account, retirement fund and no disability insurance. My life consists of experiencing adventures, meeting interesting people and doing unexpected things. I have let go of all securities.

Dream or nightmare?

The life that I lead is the result of choices I have made. I know no other lifestyle. Having spent the past eighteen years as a self-employed entrepreneur without employees, I manage to gather just enough money to live well in my own way. If I would work more, I'd earn more, but freedom and flexibility are worth more to me.
Because I have never worked for a boss, I have never known the threshold that keeps many from giving up a good steady job in exchange for their own business or adventure.
'It's easy for you,' I frequently hear people say when they hear about my adventures. 'You're alone and you don't have a responsibility towards a family.' True, I only have to take care of myself. This, too, is a choice. Of course life becomes different if you have children. But this shouldn't stop you from following your dreams.

Again, I'd like to touch upon the beautiful example of Hilda and Bas (page 46). They gave short shrift to a number of the biggest fears. They left behind everything in order to travel, not knowing what life would look like afterwards. They made a huge sailing trip with very young children. And then they started their own family business!
The moral of all stories in this book is: look at what really makes you happy, not at what generates the most money. This is confirmed by even the most successful businesspeople. In the book *Wisdom for a Young CEO*, the director of Alliant Energy Corpora-

tion shares his 'one caution – Do what makes you happy! Do not choose a direction or vocation because of money; You will only get one time around in life, and you should enjoy all of your experiences, not just your payday.'

Eef Ouwehand (page 138) watched her family business go bankrupt and did not only lose her dream job this way; she also lost her financial security. She warns, 'don't let financial security lead your decisions. This, too, can cease.'

Sir Richard Branson says that if you love what you do, money will follow. 'Money is a means of making things happen, and not an end in itself'.

In my case I spent seven years volunteering for charities, following my passion. At some point this passion shifted from 'volunteering for charities' to fighting the injustice that I came across in this world. I would have never thought that this might be financially attractive. Still, finances somehow worked out; just before I would start to get worried, I would suddenly get a freelance assignment from a consultancy agency. Ultimately, my Coins for Care experience gave me a good reputation, and now I am asked as a motivational speaker and strategic advisor. This, contrary to the charity work, does often earn me money.

If I had worked as a consultant the whole time, I could have earned more money, but I wouldn't have had this unique experience. Moreover, I would have probably not been asked so frequently as a speaker, simply because my story would have been less interesting to tell.

I can easily draw these conclusions in hindsight, but this consideration was absolutely not on my mind at that moment. I simply followed my passion. From the many interviews in this book, you'll see that almost everyone experienced things that at that moment did not seem logical, but that later turned out exactly right.

'You'll be able to connect the dots later.'

Since my book *What is Your Excuse?* was published in 2009, my life seems to have accelerated. During talks and presentations I used to always tell about the things I had done. How I had set up Coins for Care without a budget, how you can do more with less means. Now I am asked to tell about the things I do now! The book has become a business card for my lifestyle. My no-excuses mentality has generated a lot of interest. I have given a number of radio interviews, my story has been told in two books, my own book has been translated to English and I am speaking to a publisher.

I noticed that my 'excuse' book, my talks and my workshops stir people. It sets them thinking: if all this is possible, then what do I want to do with my life? I get emails from readers who tell me proudly that they quit their jobs and started their own businesses or began traveling around the world. Apparently, these themes are relevant to a lot of people.

A dream doesn't always have to be something big, by the way. You can also make more time for fun things or people that are important to you. The most important thing, I realized, is that you should be conscious of the fact that you have a choice.

I also made choices, even though they weren't very straightforward. For years I struggled with the question whether or not I should keep my house in the Netherlands. Whether or not I need a place of my own. Last year I rented out my house, which now makes me officially 'homeless'. A part of the year I live with my boyfriend on the beautiful Caribbean island of Curaçao. I have discovered that I don't need a fixed place for myself, but I would like to have my possessions within reach and not in storage, like now. The desire to discover new countries has become somewhat less; now I like returning to places and people that I already know. I can't stay in the Netherlands for too many weeks at the time, nor on Curaçao or in Miami. Diversity is what gives me energy and inspiration, so now I no longer search for the one place or the one solution that most people would see as 'normal'.

I do have to admit that lately I've become quite excited by the IKEA guide; all these smart storage systems, bookcases and chests of drawers do sometimes make me long for a place of my own, with all my things in one location... If this desire one day becomes too strong, I know I have the choice to do something to change my situation.

I have a feeling as though only now I can see my experiences from all those years in the right context. Looking back, all the strange steps I took then suddenly have a kind of logic to them. They provided the right ingredients that offer me the wonderful life I lead now. But in the past, when I was in the middle of the process, my choices often seemed far from logical! This has taught me that it is really better to let yourself be led by your feelings and intuition rather than purely by reason. In time this may bring you to a completely different place than you thought you'd end up, but it will feel good in any case.

In the end I found a good balance. I now earn my money through writing and talking about my life... and even if I tell about how I earn my money through writing and talking about my life, I still inspire people and I get paid for it! Isn't that incredible and fantastic? Who would have thought this? If I had done it for the money, I would have never landed in this unique position.

Another wonderful thing is that my bookings seem to adjust to my calendar, instead of the other way around. If I intend to go to the Netherlands for a month, I suddenly get all sorts of requests for talks exactly during that month! With the money that I earn in those few weeks, I can travel for a few months and gather new inspiration, which I pass on during my next talks.

The inspiring people I have interviewed for this book gave me new energy. It is great to know that people in different parts of the world can have a similar approach to life and head for their goals in unique ways.

Sometimes money comes by itself if you radiate enough passion. An American called Matt wanted to travel around the world. He would do a little dance at the craziest places in the world and ask someone to film it. The result is a video where passion and joy become almost tangible. It has been viewed by more than thirty million people! Greater still, when Matt returned home he was approached by a chewing gum company. They were so impressed with his video and its number of views that they offered Matt to do another trip around the world to make a second video. They would pay for all his expenses! He only had to briefly show their logo at the end of his new video. This way, Matt can continue doing what he loves most. He also inspires others (time and time again he provides me with the

best four minutes of my life!) and he gets paid for it just like that.
www.wherethehellismatt.com

Theo Jansen is a kinetic sculptor. From lightweight material he makes beautiful mechanical creatures that are moved across the beach by the wind. When he talks you can see his passion, and that he almost considers the creatures to be alive. Is he an artist or an engineer? He says the boundaries between the two only exist in our heads. At some point car manufacturer BMW asked if they could use Theo's work in an advertisement. This way, BMW now finances Theo's work. The beautiful video can be found on YouTube by searching for 'Theo Jansen, kinetic sculptor', or go directly to: http://ow.ly/250zq.
More and more freelancers let their clients decide how much they want to pay upon completion of their services. They assume that this way, they'll offer so much value, that the reward will follow as a matter of course. See Martijn Aslander (page 106).

exercise

EXERCISE:

What would you enjoy doing most if money, obligations and responsibilities would be of no importance?

If you don't quite know what makes your heart sing, you can do the following test. Stand in front of a mirror or ask a good friend to look at your face, while you talk about your various passions. Pay close attention to when your eyes start to shine and your whole face starts to beam. This is what really makes you happy!

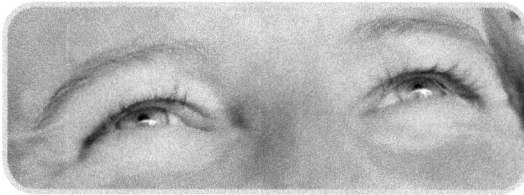

© www.eefphotography.com

Are you worried about how to combine your passion with your finances?
Then make a list with fifteen ways in which you can ultimately earn money by doing what you love. The more absurd, the better!
Now choose the three best options from this list and look at them closely. Might one of them stand a chance?

Huub (42) started his own business upon being fired from his job. He became 'dream job guru' and now helps others find their dream job.

I was working for Randstad, a temporary employment agency in the Netherlands. When they did not have my dream job there, I created a few dream positions myself! If you don't do it, who will?

The first time I became account manager for a new business in Amsterdam. I noticed that all employment agencies were fishing in the same pond and claiming the same clients. I thought: what if we think ahead and approach businesses that are planning to settle in Amsterdam; this will distinguish us, we'll have a clear added value and virtually no competition. I made a watertight plan; Randstad knew no way around it. So the idea was received well and I got the position that I had made up myself.

The second time, our office was in the absolute city center of Amsterdam. I noticed that we actually did little for the businesses that surrounded us. During an interview with AT5, a regional television station, I impulsively mentioned we should do something about this and I revealed a plan. I asked the people at AT5 to subtitle my name with 'Randstad Retail'. This Randstad division did not exist at all! The hierarchy downwards received this detail very well, but upwards the business was in a state of uproar.

Thankfully I had checked with my direct boss in advance, and he liked the idea, so he covered me. 'As long as you achieve good results it's fine by me,' he said, literally. Now 'Randstad Retail' was on television it simply existed; in short, Randstad couldn't avoid it anymore. With so much publicity something had to happen, so I was granted permission to put the plan to action.

Another while later my girlfriend decided to move to Rome. Naturally, I wanted to come with her. Randstad did have a few new branches in the north of Italy, but none in Rome. I thought to myself, actually why not in Rome?, and I wrote a business plan for 'Randstad Rome'. On my own accord, I went to Rome for a week, rented a scooter and visited all our competitors to ask for a quote for an imaginary business that would be set up in Rome. This way, I had mapped the whole market. I proposed the plan to the management. There were two things relevant to their decision to let me set up Randstad Rome. Firstly, I had already been there, I had done my research, I had shown initiative and that there is a market for Randstad. Secondly, I had already resigned so I could live in Rome with my girlfriend. Therefore, I had nothing to lose and I wasn't dependent on Randstad. In a manner of speaking, I could even choose to execute the plan myself or propose it to a competitor.

In the end, the Rome adventure did not last long. My office was part of Randstad Italy and I constantly had discussions with my Italian boss. I wanted to put the new branch on the market with a large PR offensive. He had more of a little store in mind. We did not manage to settle our differences; I was fired.

After a few years in temporary employment, I came to the conclusion that the branch of recruitment and selection is specifically focused on companies that need people. These organizations are the starting point, not the job seekers. The businesses pay for the recruitment, so they are the ones in charge.

I decided to set up a 'reversed' employment agency. We worked for our job-seeking clients. Human beings took the lead, not businesses. We tried to discover what a job seeker wanted and then found him or her a suitable job. In the end we still received a mediation fee from the company, but we would give half of it to our client as a training budget. It was a modern concept and it worked well.

I have to admit that I stepped into entrepreneurship somewhat naively. The economy was booming. All companies were looking to hire new employees and a lot of money was being paid for mediation. I quickly hired a number of people and offered them high salaries, cars and laptops. As long as things went well, this was not a problem, but in 2001, just after 9/11, everything changed. The whole recruitment and selection market collapsed; it became a huge challenge. My business with high expenses became a financial drama. I didn't turn out to be a good manager. I was thoroughly stressed and became a kind of office tyrant. When we almost went bankrupt I had to lay off my co-workers, with pain in my heart. I was left with a debt of 50,000 euros.

The same year our first child was born and on top of everything my wife turned out to have breast cancer. Thankfully everything ultimately worked out for our little family, but you can imagine how uncertain, chaotic and difficult this time was...

The debt weighed heavily on me. A good friend gave me the tip to make arrangements with my creditors. I didn't even know this was possible, but in unusual situations, many businesses prefer receiving a small amount immediately, rather than a larger amount in the future (with the risk that the person who must pay them may go bankrupt, meaning they won't get a thing). Training office De Baak allowed me to redeem my debt by providing trainings. This way, I managed to pay off a large part of my debt.

In this period I came up with a new idea. I wanted to give trainings to job seekers and let them pay for it themselves. This made me independent from large corporations and I would be able to focus even more on my clients. I had learned from my experiences and decided not to hire people this time around. This posed fewer risks and moreover, I had proven to be a bad manager.

At TalentFirst we only work with Friend-chisers, who completely commit themselves to the concept and the trainings we give. It is great that everyone has their own responsibilities, they can manage their time flexibly, have their own clients, and still, we have a common philosophy, method and space.

I am actually thankful that things went the way they did. If the crisis had arrived a year later, things would have gone very differently. I would have had even more people employed, had even higher costs and the financial disaster would have been even bigger. I probably wouldn't have survived the crisis, then. It may sound strange, but such a crisis is good for entrepreneurs. If the economy is going well, there is less pressure. Crisis is an opportunity. A chance for taking a good look at your costs and your value. If you earn money easily, you won't pay much attention to it and you become clumsy and lazy.

What I have learned is that you should take as much action as you can. You should plant as many seeds as you can, and create and optimize all circumstances that are within your control. Then you have to let go and leave your success to the universe. Don't take things personally. Even if you really did everything you could, it still doesn't always work out. But then at least you can't blame yourself.

© www.fotolemaire.nl

Tips from Huub:

It is possible!

Imagine these two scenarios: 1) what happens without action? 2) what happens if you do take action?

Make sure that as many people as possible know what you want. Involve them with your dream. Communicate in as many ways as you can 1) what you want to achieve and 2) what your unique qualities are.

Are you having trouble putting this into words? Then ask the people around you for help. For them it is easier; they see you better than you see yourself. Ask a large number of friends, family members, colleagues and even your boss to answer the question of what you have to offer. You can also ask them what makes you unique. You'll see that many people will list the same characteristics. Make a list with the ten most important, unique ones.

Inform your boss and your colleagues. For sure: you should tell your boss! Don't let your boss be the last to know.

Think BIG! Timothy Ferris (author of The 4-Hour Workweek) says that it is often easier to realize big dreams than to realize small ones. Big dreams are more remarkable and inspiring and they give you more adrenalin. Moreover you distinguish yourself, which gives you a lot less competition. Forget the question: 'what do I want?' Many people find it paralyzing. Instead, it's better to ask: 'what do I have to offer?' This is more concrete, and it can be tested and put to action.

If you know what you have to offer, you know what you can mean to others. This way you can start partnerships. A new job is a sort of partnership. You offer something to the business and the business offers something to you. If you start looking at it in this way, as an equal partnership, you suddenly become an attractive partner for a business.

Definitely DON'T do this:

X Pretend to be someone you're not.

X Remain reserved (as others will magnify your modesty)

The process that you go through when you want to realize your dream can roughly be divided into three steps:
1) Insight: what is your dream and which of your talents will help you realize it?
2) Translation: communicate your dream and transform it into action points.
3) Action: step-by-step work your way down your to-do list.

X Don't turn to action too quickly; take care to complete steps one and two. But don't spend too much time preparing, either, as nothing will happen this way.

www.huubvanzwieten.nl

Choose consciously what you spend your time and money on

Some people spend money they don't have to buy things they don't want to impress people they don't like.

If you've got an idea of what you want to achieve, you'll frequently be confronted with obstacles. You want to make a faraway journey or take a sabbatical, but you don't have money. You want to take that particular course, or start your own business, but you don't have time.

In order to start heading towards your dream, you must first clear the way.

Most people find time and money the most limiting factors. They think: if only I had more time and/or money, then I would be able to follow my dream.

I have realized that the decision is yours how you spend your scarce amount of time and money. Only you are often not aware that there is a choice, or that you made a choice.

For example, Katharine Hepburn stopped making movies at the peak of her career in order to spend more time with her son. Many people would have never considered the option, but she realized that she had a choice and consequently she made that choice. She never regretted it.

If you want to work less, there are two options: save up in advance (meaning you'll have to work longer) in order to keep up the same spending pattern or make sure that your expenses go down.

Why not spend a month keeping track of what you spend your money on. What strikes you? Are there expenses you could easily avoid? Instead of eating out, you could cook your friends a dinner at home. A cozy solution. Do you often have coffee out? Calculate what you could save if you would drink coffee at a friend's place or bring a thermos, and consider what you could do with this money. Are all your insurances really needed? And you can read the newspaper online. And so on.

Instead of buying expensive presents you could create your presents yourself.

For example, I sometimes paint the name of a newborn baby on a piece of driftwood as an original and personal present. It's fun to vent your creativity again. Or instead of an expensive present you can give friends a 'voucher' on which you offer to babysit their children some evening. This will give them quality time together and you will get to know their children better.

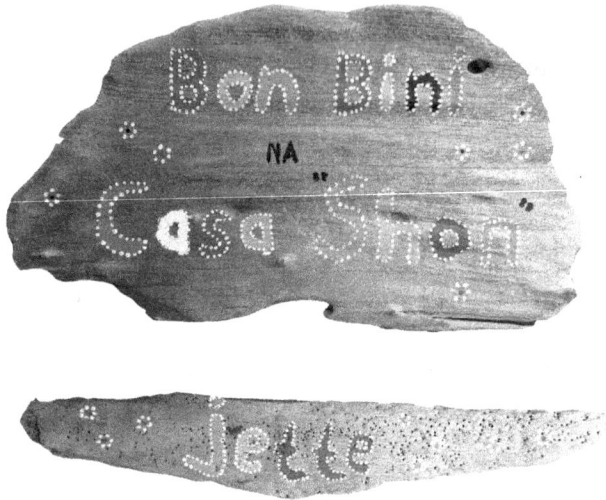

I never considered television to be very important. Years ago, when I discovered how much time watching television drained, I resolutely got rid of it. Not once did I regret this. It creates plenty of time for other things. If I now walk through town and I see all those anonymous bodies slouched in front of their TVs, I sometimes think: is this what these people truly want? Or is it a habit? Something they do from indecisiveness, fatigue, or maybe even depression?

Unfortunately I've noticed that I do spend a lot of time at my computer and this is also a kind of addiction. If you have access to the internet, there's always a mountain of emails waiting to be answered, and things to see, read, learn or discover.

On the yacht in the Caribbean we would sometimes be without internet for days. As long as I had reception, I would feverishly spend hours behind my computer. Soon it will be impossible, and then I'll miss all sorts of things, I would think, stressed out. No email, Skype or Twitter, no chance to look up anything.

But as soon as we'd lose reception, something special would happen. Suddenly I'd have seas of time. This gave me inspiration and I could write. I realized that my 'internet addiction' cost me my inspiration. Plus, it slurped several hours of my day that I could have also spent on other things.

When it comes to money, over the course of time I have made some clear choices. I will name a few; maybe they will inspire you, too, to get your finances in order.

> I focused on what was truly important to me: **communication**. This is why, as a student already, I decided that my phone and travel costs should never hinder me in doing what I really wanted. Both privately as well as professionally. Calling someone, going somewhere? I will never say 'no' because of the costs. Otherwise I would miss a lot of fun things, and professionally I would be taken less seriously. Just imagine what would have happened if, when I was setting up Coins for Care, I would have to tell a potential sponsor, 'would you mind calling me back? You see I'm calling by mobile,' or when I had finally found a store chain prepared to place collection boxes, I had answered, 'sorry, I can't go to meet you as Rotterdam is a bit too far for me...'

> If you're an entrepreneur, **insurance agents** will try to make you afraid of unforeseen circumstances, and then they'll offer you options for covering these risks. They'll try to sell you all sorts of insurances. Disability insurances, pension insurances, and so on. If I wanted to cover all those risks, I would have to earn twice as much (and therefore work twice as much) as I do now. I have consciously chosen to work just enough to live off, not

the other way around. Take a good look at which insurances you really need and which ones you don't. It also helps having all your insurances with the same company. Sometimes you'll get discounts this way, and you'll avoid unnecessary overlaps.

My biggest expenses are **travel tickets**. And I believe that every dollar I spend on a flight is spent well. When I go somewhere else, I always live very cheaply. I stay in hostels or sleep over at friends' houses. But in order to get there, you sometimes need to spend a little.

I collect experiences, not material things or money. Clothing, makeup, cars, furniture, CDs, magazines and other 'luxury goods' don't charm me. I try to resist the temptation to just buy things. I notice that when I walk through a city, I am automatically drawn to the stores. The whole atmosphere is designed to say, 'buy me,' or even, 'you need me'. Therefore, I will only go shopping if I really need something. If I feel an irresistible urge to buy something, I will first sleep on it. If I still want it the next day, I will buy it, otherwise I won't. How much do you spend on impulsive purchases?

Going out (e.g. for dinner) can have quite an impact on your budget. I believe it is important to have a good time with friends. And as it happens, this often takes place in restaurants and bars. I personally don't drink alcohol and I don't smoke, and when I compare my expenses with friends, it is a fraction of their budget. I have discovered that even the most expensive restaurants always have affordable options on the menu. So there's always a choice. However, it is always a bit unfortunate for those who watch their budget when, after a luxurious meal with lots of alcohol and expensive dishes, their friends decide to split the bill...

Of course, there's always the option of inviting friends to your house. Cooking **together** or taking turns hosting a dinner is fun, more personal and a lot cheaper.

➤ Who knows there may be others who would like to consume a bit less; together you can propose these options to your friends.

➤ My plea is not to live frugally; it is to make **clear choices** for what you find important.

➤ Say you want to make a trip and you have no money for it, but you do drink two cans of Red Bull a day (I seriously once overheard two girls on the beach complain that it cost so much money per month) or you buy sandwiches instead of bringing a home packed lunch. For the amount of money that you would save on this yearly, you would easily be able to pay a ticket to wherever in the world you want!

exercise

EXERCISE:

The first step in the direction of more time and money is to pay attention to how you now deal with these important factors.

For the duration of a few weeks (preferably a month), take notes on what you spend your time and money on.

Make two separate overviews: one for time and one for money. You can also keep track of time one month and money the other. The principle is the same for both. Keep track of everything; also fifteen minutes or a dollar per day will amount to something substantial per month. Don't be discouraged! Your only task is to make an overview; not to change anything. In a month you'll make totals, you'll try to rubricate and you'll analyze the overview.

Maybe the following questions can help you:

- What strikes you first?
- Which matters take up the largest portion of your money or time?
- What kind of spending surprises you?
- Can you see certain patterns?
- Which matters are truly important to you?
- How much time do you spend in front of the television? On the internet? On domestic tasks that you could also outsource?
- What kind of spending didn't you expect and/or may not be worth it? Mark them.
- Which things give you energy and which things cost energy?
- Do you spend enough time on your dream?

Now ask yourself how you can best make time and/or money available for your dream. Are there certain things you can leave out completely? Things you can outsource or replace with something less expensive or time-consuming? If you can save ten percent on a large item, it can already make a large difference.

Don't ask what the world needs.

Find out what makes you come

alive,

and then go out and do it.

What the world needs is

people who have come alive.

– Howard Thurman –

© Laura Weyl

Artist Michaelangelo (28) lives like a sort of gypsy in California, without a job, a fixed place to live or other certainties. He lives off and for his stories, music and drawings.

The winner of the storytelling competition had told her audience about the first time she kissed a penis. The second prize went to a young man whose story was called 'coke dick', so that was about how he couldn't get it up. The third prize went to the story of a vegan woman who got home drunk in a stupor one night and ate a pound of raw bacon that belonged to her housemate...

The tradition of The Bard seemed to have been lost. So there I stood, with my story about how I allied coyotes in the desert, and about how later they guided me through the land of the dead to teach me important life lessons.

You frequently hear people say that they are following their dreams, but how many people literally do? Who still dares truly to be led by sub- or unconscious visions?

I am someone who literally follows his dreams, and stories are just about the only things I own. Well, I do own a few other things as well, but they're mostly tools by which to usher these stories into the world: a computer, a few microphones, a camera, some musical instruments, and also drawing and painting materials. But if it should come down to it, I wouldn't even need those things; my words, my voice and my animated body language would be enough to let my stories propel themselves.

**'look hear, there's nothing here; we can make
things disappear and reappear at will.
there's nothing here now, still.
hear now, still here now.'**

I've been hallucinating ever since I was a child; I often have waking dreams and visions. I actually don't think this is very strange. In fact, our thoughts and memories are also like hallucinations. They're imaginative visualizations of otherwise invisible energetic processes that sometimes even reflect our (wishes for the) future. As an artist I study these processes and images and analyze them for archetypical, anecdotic and practical information.

As a child I had an imaginary friend who would colorfully appear before me, dressed in her safari outfit. Pietie would take me on safari and would teach me all sorts of things. She was so real to me that I even convinced my parents to place an extra plate on the table for her.

Psychologists might say that my parents' divorce and the tensions at home were the cause of my introversion, that I escaped reality with the help of an *imaginary* friend.

I see a different cause, but it's true, I did retreat by means of my creative obsessions. I only watched nature documentaries, read a lot about animals, and this was all I talked about. Then it was drawing and painting--animals, still--that made up my entire world. By the time I was nine or ten, photography was my obsession and I would often be in the forest before sunrise to be greeted by deer, which I would immortalize in the light of my passion. A few years later film was It for me, and you would frequently find me in Amsterdam's theater cafés, the twelve-year-old paparazzo, hunting for famous faces in the same manner as I had captured the likeness of well-known animals during a South African safari the year before. Later still, I set aside my camera, paintbrushes and passion for the animal kingdom, and I began writing film scripts. I helped, amongst others, my school friend David Verbeek (whose newest film is showing during the Cannes International Film Festival) with his film projects.

You could say that when my childhood imaginary friend left and the extra dinner plate was put back in the cupboard, she was internalized as the thought-form of my anima, my internal muse. And in these various creative disciplines I found different techniques for traveling inward and re-establishing contact with that animaginary friend.

When I finished High School, I went to my father in Florida with the intention to study film in New York. In order to move there, my father said, I should first have some money as a buffer, so I took a job at a pawnshop in Miami. Around the same time I fell in love with a girl in whom I recognized the imaginary muse that I had for years pursued in many forms.

I discovered marijuana, which opened my mind's eye and gave me new inspiration to paint. My outlook is that we can learn from plants and animals what it is to be human. This was why I, at some point, worked with the shamanic, psycho-active plant Ayahuasca, in among other places Brazil; in order to generate new visions. The way in which these colorful visions bloomed before my inner eye and the way in which it guided me through an uncharted psyche-safari reminded me of how I had experienced my *imaginary* friend as a child.

This is where the story actually starts; how I became an artist and how a unique world view was formed. I started to consider my life as a kind of cinematic narrative; a film in which I am my own author, director, actor, and composer, in collaboration with allies. Whether it can be called life-art or madness, is up for consideration. In any case I'm leaving behind my 'pre-posthumous' publications in the shape of paintings, writings and musical compositions, the imaginative footprints of a wakeful wanderer in pursuit of a vision...

I literally followed my dreams, visions and feelings. When I was nineteen I moved back to the Netherlands, without a plan but with my girlfriend, in order to further our art there. We landed in a large anti-squat near a luxurious shopping street in Amsterdam where we lived for next to nothing. We were constantly very lucky. For example, a lady next-door wanted to toss her old painting supplies but ended up giving them to us.

Next, we moved to North Carolina. After three years in the mountains, we both decided to go our own ways. I gave up my job at a sandwich bar and headed to San Francisco. When I arrived there I was unprepared, as usual. I had simply begun traveling in order to put my almost irrational optimism and trust in my gifts to the test under the motto: 'At ease, let yourself fall, and a net will form to catch you.'

And so it was that from the very beginning I was invited to live in the houses of other creative individuals, because my lifestyle inspired them. I was offered a free studio space above a cafe. Twice I painted a huge mural in a restaurant, in exchange for accommodation and food. Unfortunately the first time we disagreed on the compensation and my enormous work was whitewashed away within a few months. Sadly this also happened with the second mural because the restaurant was sold.

Despite these kinds of emotional setbacks, I always went on and transformed my approach. The time was ripe again to change my medium, and I became a musician. I'd never had any musical schooling but I do always hear music in my head (you may call this a delusion, but if you're able to externalize it, its hard not to acknowledge it as real). I began recording vocal compositions under the name TheaTerRa and this drew the attention of another traveling dreamer, a guitarist from Israel, with whom I set up the band Morph Dwarf. My friend Benny used my 'vanished' mural as his album cover. This felt like reincarnation. Nowadays I strive after my eternity, with aid of multimedia, without ever actually exhausting my lust for expression.

Occasionally I earn some money, either by helping with moving or as a photographer. But for me, money is a means that helps me swing from one liana of freedom and creativity to another. Occasionally I find a roommate and we rent a room together, or I sleep over at the same place for a prolonged period of time. A temporary 'permanent' place to live is necessary in order to rest and process all the movement, but it can also become claustrophobic. I am aware that too much comfort stifles my creative flow. When I move within the world, I can clearly see my inner stillness. When I stay comfortably in the same place, my worldly thoughts are in motion and my environment is still.

What do I want to be when I grow up? Realistically, naturally... myself.

www.voidandimagination.com

195

Think positively and visualize

During my interview with Huub (page 176), he proudly shared that he had recently lost twelve kilos in weight. He had wanted this for a long time, but he had never succeeded until now. Then how did he do it?

'I knew what I had to do in order to lose weight, but I didn't have the motivation (yet),' Huub explained. 'Then I saw a video by Anthony Robbins on TED.com and I realized that it is possible, it is really possible to transform your body in a few months. I imagined what my life would look like if I could manage to lose weight and what it would look like if I couldn't manage this. In both cases I tried to visualize what my work, my friendships and my relationship would look like in one, five and ten years. What would my self-image be like? How would I feel? I very closely explored the positive and the negative scenarios and in my mind I experienced both situations; the dream and the drama. Of course it quickly became apparent that I would feel much better, in every respect, if I could make my goal, assume a healthy lifestyle and lose the excess weight. Then I entered the third phase: no more excuses! "What's keeping you?" I asked myself. Then I just started. From one day to the next. No effort whatsoever. I simply didn't feel like a cake, even if someone put it right in front of me. I knew what I wanted to achieve and a cake just did not fit the picture.'

A similar practice has been used all over the world for thousands of years. Various religions, gurus and ordinary people use visualization techniques: they create an image of what they want to achieve, and by doing so, they increase the chances of it becoming reality.

Practically speaking this means that you may want to steer your thoughts to positive images. For example, if you're afraid you may have a parking ticket, you'll be thinking of the ticket constantly. Then chances are that you will indeed find a ticket on your windshield when you return to your car.

It is better to visualize a clear windshield and create a good feeling with it, so you'll think of untroubled parking instead of the ticket.

To make a long story short: a few years ago *The Secret* was an enormous hype. The book and the movie revealed the long-kept secret of success. In fact, the secret is no more and no less than the previous story, but then somewhat popularized.

A friend of mine was constantly talking about the 'groundbreaking' technique of *The Secret* and I thought: is it really that groundbreaking? I've been applying the principle for years and I think many others have as well...

Be as it may, I was in Curaçao for the first time in years and I had spent three weeks having a tremendous time. Unfortunately the end of my stay had come near, and this particular friend suggested watching *The Secret* together. Why not, I thought. Always good to be reminded of ancient wisdom. But the movie was so over the top, with exaggerated testimonials and pretentious academic explanations, that I fell asleep on the couch after ten minutes...

Yet somehow that evening, something must have been set in motion by talking about visualization. The next morning I decided to make my last day in Curaçao unforgettable. My last sailing lesson was in the morning, and when it was over, my instructor allowed me to use the boat longer, so I could continue practicing until I literally had no strength left in my arms. 'At least I made the absolute most of it!' I then sighed, exhausted but satisfied.

All my friends had to work that day, unfortunately, but I had agreed to have lunch with a friend who worked in a store by the beach. After a fun lunch meeting I began feeling muscle aches as expected and I thought: a massage would be more than welcome. I could almost feel the hands of the masseur on my aching muscles. I stepped out of the store, onto the beach, and to my surprise there was a massage tent right in front of me that I had never seen before! The masseur happened to have time and so it was that I had a wonderful massage.

Meanwhile I became aware that it was indeed a perfect last day: sailing, lunch followed by a massage; how could I wish for more. Only one minor thing inadvertently flashed through my mind: it was a shame nobody had time to do something fun in the afternoon. Then my phone rang: 'My work has been canceled, do you feel like some wakeboarding?' a friend of mine asked. You bet!

The whole afternoon he taught me wakeboarding at a beautiful part of the Spanish Water Bay. When we were about to return to the port, he asked if I felt like a swim by a deserted beach. Of course I did! While we floated in the clear blue water, I again reflected on my day. I told my friend I had really had a fantastic holiday and that I had done everything I had dreamed of, and more. The only thing I hadn't done, not that it mattered, I explained, was scuba diving. It was the end of the day, the sun was setting. My departure was the next morning, so diving just wouldn't happen, I knew.

And then something strange happened. At that very moment we saw a man walk out of the water. He simply walked onto the beach, no land in sight, wearing clothes and a hat! My friend and I looked at each other as though we saw a mirage. To complete our perplexity, the strange man approached us, confused, and asked us in broken English, 'where am I?' We thought it was a joke, but quickly the man, who turned out to be from Hungary, explained that he worked on a cruise ship and it was his day off; he wanted to avoid the tourists. He had started to walk along the coastline, and when this became impossible, he continued on swimming, until he had reached our beach. We offered the guy a lift in our boat, back to civilization. I asked him what kind of work he did on the cruise ship and he answered, 'I'm a diving instructor'. And while a little voice in my head cried, 'what a coincidence! Weren't we just talking about diving?' he continued, 'I'm still planning on making a night dive before the ship leaves, you two want to join?'

It sounds almost too good to be true, but I unconsciously managed to apply the principles of visualization, at the last moment, to round off my dream holiday with something that would have seemed impossible.

Think of what this could mean for you and your dream. What do you want to achieve? Allow yourself to dream a little and visualize that you have actually made your dreams come true. There's no harm in trying this. Dream little dreams, or dream big! The most important thing is to think positively about what you want to achieve and not about what you want to avoid. The universe apparently doesn't know the word 'no'. See yourself tread the world you long for. Feel the experience of sitting at the desk of your own business, or imagine doing absolutely nothing in a hammock.

It can't do any harm and it may do some good, I'd say. Barbara Ehrenreich does warn us for the risks of applying this principle wrongly. See the short video with her story and fantastic live cartoon illustrations: http://ow.ly/29lkY.

I am not the only one who puts this principle into practice. Eef (page 138) says, 'your attitude is important. For my internship on Curaçao, I received 750 Netherlands Antillean guilders for a state allowance. The house I had rented, however, cost me 1750 Antillean guilders. I will always remember my mother's reaction when I shared my worries with her. She said, "Then you had better make sure you will earn that money!" Back in the Netherlands I am again renting a (too) expensive house. My attitude is: I will simply earn the money. And I have managed to do this for years now.'

Huub (page 176), author of a book on visualization, wrote in his blog: *I'm walking through the artistic district of Amsterdam, the Jordaan,* where I live; it is also the setting of my book. At a sandwich bar a tourist nudges me, pointing at a picture of Marcel Wanders on the wall. 'Is that you?' Funny, I think, because I had been planning to walk by Wanders' gallery. Perhaps I'll even run into him, because I had never met him before and it was still on my bucket list. The man was apparently already in my thoughts if someone thinks we look like each other. Wanders appears in my book with the inspiring text, 'I don't have a wish list; if I want something I simply do it.' A magical attitude to life!

I walk towards the gallery with a delicious sandwich and – no surprises here – Marcel Wanders is nowhere in sight. I do see a beautiful piece of art, headed by the word 'Bloemgracht', which is the street I live in and the exact setting of my book (in the yet-to-be-realized DreamJobHotel above our home...). While eating my sandwich I walk outside; across the street and into the sun. Suddenly a newspaper is blown in my direction from the terrace of a bar. The newspaper lands right in front of my feet. I follow my intuition, grab the newspaper and I walk to the terrace so I can return the paper to the person who had been reading it. I hand over the paper. It's Marcel Wanders.

I turn around while this bizarre fact sinks in. It can't be true. This is it. This is the magic!

I instantly turn towards him and I excuse myself for interrupting. I introduce myself and tell him that exactly a year ago I had written a book in which he appears, and that I would still love to offer it to him. I also tell him how bizarre the situation is: my book covers exactly the phenomenon of life's magic when you follow your intuition and let the universe do the rest. He lets me know how I can reach him; he looks forward to make an appointment with me. It really works! Life's magic will unfold if you're open to it. Wow!

Visualizing your success doesn't only work for airy-fairy types of people. On the following page, Iko, an engineer, shares how he applies this principle. His approach is, 'be open to coincidences, but also take initiatives yourself.'

Sow a thought, reap an action,
Sow an action, reap a habit,
Sow a habit, reap a character,
Sow a character, reap a destiny.
– Seneca –

Iko (37) follows his dreams: from Nigeria to Peru to Curaçao; from electrical engineering to management consulting; from development aid to sailing school. Every few years he changes his dreams. He learned to follow his intuition and trusts he'll find the right things.

As a child I already wanted to be an engineer, just like my father and my two brothers. So I went to study electrical engineering. I think I was socially predestined to do this.

In elementary school I thought that middle school and then high school would be more interesting. When I ended up there I hoped that university would be 'it'. In university I figured it would happen in the business world. But I noticed that normal people are everywhere, they all have their shortcomings, and you don't have to look up to them.

I wanted to go abroad as soon as I could. Adventure drew me. I began working for Shell. After the internal training I was allowed to indicate my preference. I said I was open for any suggestion, only I didn't want to stay in the Netherlands and I didn't want to do research. I would have loved to go to Nigeria; this seemed exciting. But Shell only had one post there which had already been filled. To my surprise I was stationed in Rijswijk, the Netherlands, at the research department! When I asked my planner about this, he said, 'if I thought your opinion was important, I would have asked for it.' Or something along those lines. I was flabbergasted.

After three weeks I ran into a young woman whom I had met at the internal training. She told me she had been the one selected for the post in Nigeria, but her partner was unhappy with this. 'I just told my boss that I'm not going,' she confided to me. I thought about this. Her planner was probably quite upset about this. I decided to call and tell him I wanted to go to Nigeria. He was indeed very happy to have found a replacement so quickly.

Four weeks later I was in Nigeria. I had no idea what I was going to earn. Money wasn't my concern, but it turned out to be quite a bit. In the beginning everything was exciting, but after a while life became a routine. For example, I would first have to spend a year working on an oil platform in order to gain experience for the office work for which I was actually hired. But after eight months it started feeling wrong. The atmosphere on the platform was not good. I had gained the experience necessary and asked to be transferred to the office, which was granted. Very soon afterwards, the oil platform was raided and the new supervisor was kidnapped. If I had still worked there, this would have been my destiny!

The office work in Nigeria was one big show. I was already approached by people presenting their 'final' reports on my first day as the leader of a large project that would take ten months! They didn't even have the correct data from me yet... How could they have produced a 'final' report? It was mostly politics and this was not what I wanted.

Meanwhile, my Peruvian girlfriend, whom I had met during our studies in France, decided she wanted to return to Peru. I feared that our relationship would not survive an even bigger distance, so I quit my job and went after her. Together we decided to begin exporting textiles. For a few months we traveled through the country, searching for cheap producers from small villages. Ironically, a large producer in Lima, Peru's capital, turned out to be the cheapest. So our travels had not been necessary, although they had been fun.

Through word of mouth I searched for buyers in the Netherlands. I told everyone what I was doing. A former fellow student turned out to have in-laws in the textile industry who were glad to help.

Unfortunately my girlfriend and I still broke up. It had a huge emotional impact on me and I moved back to the Netherlands.

I decided to apply for a job at a prestigious strategic management consultancy. I thought it would be fun to work hard, learn a lot and keep myself busy with international projects. A brilliant former fellow student, much smarter than me, was rejected by them. I went to him for advice and he told me about the difficult case they had presented him with. I thought: it would be quite a coincidence if they use the same case on me, and subsequently I locked myself up in the library for three days to learn all I could about that particular case. It was incredible, but my last job interview with them was with the same partner and case as my friend! I was accepted.

Meanwhile, I became more and more aware of the fact that I had to pay extra attention to these coincidences. If you voice your intention, just like with Nigeria, chance will be on your side, but you do have to take action yourself. If I hadn't spent three days in the library, I would have probably also been rejected, just like my friend. If you don't show initiative, nothing will happen.

The first four months of working for the consultancy were a lot of fun. After that, it was mostly stressful. We often worked till midnight, sometimes even longer. Consultants are, in fact, insecure overachievers who try to stay in control by making longer hours. I noticed that the stress was giving my colleagues physical symptoms; I started to experience them, too. However, as I had gone through all that trouble to get the job, I wanted to complete the year. I managed to do this, but not a day longer...

After some time in the business world, I wanted something else. Everyone appeared to think it was so important what we did: making a business a tad more efficient, helping an organization to earn just a bit more money. But I didn't find it very useful, and not worth being stressed and suffering health problems for.

I wanted to do something useful and decided I wanted to work for Doctors Without Borders. I actually wanted to be a project coordinator, but this meant I'd have to spend a while doing project logistics first. I was sent out to Zambia. After three months, the project coordinator there was fired and I was asked to take over her tasks...

The work was hard, but I considered it useful and it fulfilled me. The people are happy that you're there and your colleagues are also motivated. What I learned at Doctors Without Borders is that helping others in concrete ways can really make you happy.

My second project was in Mexico. My job was to close down the project and fire people. This was less fun. My third project was in the Democratic Republic of Congo. This was plain dangerous.

After a year and a half of very intensive work, with hardly any days off, I simply wanted to relax. I felt I had experienced what it was all about. Time for something else.

I was born in Curaçao, where I lived until the age of six. I thought it might be fun to start a catamaran sailing school there. I was quite good at sailing, but I'd only ever been on a catamaran once in my life. Again, 'coincidentally', an opportunity came onto my path.

I was staying over with friends in Curaçao who took me to a party. I told one of the guests about my plans. To my surprise he said that his son was a catamaran instructor looking for a job! I had found my partner. Not long after that we found a location, and when I look back now, I think this was enormously lucky, as all beaches are usually 'already taken'.

I put all my savings of the last few years into Cat Sailing. I loved the sailing school. The act of sailing and the sea never tired me. I also noticed that you meet a large amount of great people this way. This was really what I wanted to do!

But at a given moment I was through with this, too. Three years later I'd been there, done that, and I wanted to go on. I realized that I enjoyed starting things, but the moment it became a routine, I considered it to be boring.

While I was setting up my sailing school, I was evicted from my rental home. I had little money to spare but I wanted to buy my own house, and therefore I found a house that needed to be renovated, with extra rooms that I could rent out to interns. I had enjoyed the renovations so much that after I sold Cat Sailing, I searched for another house in need of a facelift, this time with the purpose of turning it into a low budget guesthouse. I began telling everyone. And again I very quickly found a perfect house.

When I had bought the first house, I had no idea how I wanted to do it up. I wasn't a handyman. The garden in itself was already filled with waste and other rubbish, so my mission actually seemed impossible. At that moment a Colombian man cycled by, stopped and asked, 'do you have any work for me?' He helped me with the garden and also turned out to be able to lay bricks...

A few years later, when I had bought the guesthouse, I again needed help. And who just happened to be cycling past, again?

At this moment, my dream is setting up a Bed & Breakfast, and this is keeping me busy right now. I would enjoy organizing frequent spiritual courses there, along the lines of 'cool' meditation and personal development. This still needs to crystallize a little. I never plan too far ahead. As long as I'm enjoying it, I'll stay in Curaçao.

Iko's tips

Making decisions does not mean making a list of pros and cons. It's more like a pyramid: the most important thing to you will be on top. The rest is irrelevant.

Act in accordance with what you want to achieve. Formulate your goals clearly, make plans and pay attention to chance.

You won't realize your dreams with excuses such as 'yes, but...' and 'only if...' If you do that, you're guaranteed never to arrive where you want to be...

My most important tip is: just get started! Do it!

Don't be afraid to fail

Face your biggest fears!

Unfortunately, in our culture, we are raised with the intention to make as few mistakes as possible. In school, any errors were crossed out by a red marker and all attention went to what we did well. This is how it should be; this is how you must do it. Above all, we had to color between the lines. Nobody will teach you how to make mistakes. There is no support for the 'misguided ones' who color outside the lines. While you actually learn most from making mistakes. Think about your own life. What has made the biggest impression on you? It is probably something that you tried hard and failed to achieve.

Imagine trying to catch a cat by the tail… This is something you might try once and then you'll know it's not the right way. Nobody will have to explain this to you again.

We should actually give each other more space for trying out things and taking risks. Almost all big discoveries were made 'accidentally', when another experiment actually failed…

There is a reason why there are so many catchy quotes about failing and success by famous scientists, philosophers, politicians and marketers.

"There is no failure, only feedback."
˜ Robert Allen

There are no **failures**, only **unintended results**

Many people let themselves be held back because they are afraid to fail. Martijn (page 106) says he actually always seeks out challenges, faces his fears and confronts himself.

If the worst thing you can think of really takes place, you may notice that it is actually not so bad.

'Stability is an illusion.'

– Seth Godin –

For years, one of my biggest fears was to be stranded without food. I ate every two hours; otherwise I'd start feeling weak and shaky. I always carried a lunchbox with cheese sandwiches with me or at least some muesli bars. Then I spontaneously decided to participate in the adventurous TV program *Survivor*. Together with Marnix (page 70) I was confined in an abandoned cave.

We didn't eat more than half a fist of cooked rice per day and if we had managed to catch something that day, we'd have some fish. After three days of hardly eating anything I got sick. I felt weak and lightheaded and I had the feeling I could faint any moment. 'This is exactly what I was so afraid of,' I explained to Marnix. I ate some more rice and decided to step out of the program if the nasty feeling persisted. However, a few hours later I started feeling better and, strangely enough, I had no problems whatsoever in the weeks that followed! Apparently your body quickly adapts. This was a liberating feeling. My worst nightmare had come true and it had only made me stronger!

Another interesting point is that I was a vegetarian when I started *Survivor* and I was dreading having to eat fish. Now I have to admit that the snails (without herb butter...) did not appeal to me much, but after the adventure I did start eating fish, which opened up a world for me.

Another common fear is to end up in a strange country without any money. It happened to me in Madagascar. I had been in South Africa for a while and decided to make a big dream come true: to travel around in Madagascar for a month. I bought a ticket and landed on the beautiful though primitive island without a plan, without a guide and with only thirty dollars in cash. Because I had been able to withdraw money everywhere in South Africa, I did have two debit cards and two credit cards with me. And then I found out that there is not a single ATM on Madagascar!

There I was, at the airport. I didn't even have enough money for a taxi to a bank in the capital, where I hoped to withdraw money with my credit card. I caught a ride from the Hilton Hotel bus, where a South African businessman approached me. He said he had overheard me speak French and he asked if I wanted to translate his meeting, because his interpreter had called in sick at the last moment. I promised I'd help and told him about my financial situation. 'Then I'll book you a room for tonight at the Hilton and I'll organize a taxi to take you to the bank tomorrow,' the businessman promised. He kept his word. I translated his meeting and the next day I went to the bank, where it turned out that you could only withdraw cash with a Visa card. I had two MasterCards... Finally I found out there was one possibility, but it would involve waiting 48 hours for my money. I spent the next two days helping the businessman with a few things for his project and he paid my hotel room and food. When I got my money, I went my way to discover the magnificent country.

A few weeks later I was in a tiny village by the sea and I had to go south in order to travel onwards. However, there was no road leading in that direction. Flying would involve first heading north for a long stretch, which seemed illogical to me. Plus, I didn't have enough money for a plane ticket.

I asked local fishermen if they could take me south. 'Depending on the wind that will take a week to ten days and it will be extremely expensive,' they warned me. I asked how much it would cost and they replied gravely, 'thirty dollars!' This was about the amount of money I had left, so I decided to risk it.

What followed was one of the most beautiful traveling experiences in my life. We sailed for a week along the coastline, in a hollow tree trunk with an improvised mast and a sail made of cloth, all held together by some sticks and ropes. We slept on deserted beaches and ate fish that we caught ourselves. Finally I arrived in a village with some more tourists, where a Frenchman completely unknown to me lent me a few hundred dollars. Of course I paid him back after my trip and we are still friends.

I would not have experienced all these things if I had had enough cash on me. However, I would not have wanted to miss any of these adventures. Having no money in a strange country is not very scary, after all. It offers new possibilities and unusual experiences!

You will get an enormous amount of energy if you try something new or exciting and push your own boundaries. Adriaan (page 84) says he is frequently nervous before being interviewed. When the media turn out to portray his give-me-a-spaceflight initiative positively, he feels so happy that it seems as though he is already in space at that very moment!

According to Shakespeare, 'cowards die many times before their deaths; the valiant never taste of death but once. Why would you always be afraid?'

When Eef's family business went bankrupt (page 138), Eef realized that even a history of one hundred and four years doesn't offer any certainties. The bankruptcy put an end to Eef's dream to follow in her father's footsteps. But at the same time, it was the start of a new dream. Her move to Curaçao and her decision to return a year later, too, fall in the category: it isn't a failure, it's a choice. 'I now know that I can always start again and I am not afraid of it; I find it exciting!' Eef says. 'I've learned from this. I am very flexible. I can start a new life anywhere, no problem. I'm learning more and more to let go of certainties.'

'What doesn't kill me makes me stronger,' was originally a quote by Friedrich Nietzsche. Nowadays you'll frequently hear the words in many song lyrics.

Inventor Thomas Edison became famous, amongst other things, because of the improvements he made to light bulbs. For a year and a half he systematically experimented with any thinkable material to see what gave the best light without burning down. Finally he found the right conducting wire. This had taken a certain kind of attitude. Edison said, 'I have not failed. I've just found 10,000 ways that did not work.'

So if you have an idea, don't let yourself be held back by a fear that you may fail. Imagine what it will feel like if you do succeed. And then think of a worst-case scenario where things don't go as planned. At least you will have learned something and you can always decide to try again, possibly in a different way or at another moment.

'Success consists of going from failure to failure without loss of enthusiasm.'

– Sir Winston Churchill –

There will always be people who'll say, 'you shouldn't have tried that,' or 'didn't I tell you?' But many others will admire your courage and they'll maybe even be inspired to also take that exciting first step in the direction of their dream.

In a beautiful poem, Theodore Roosevelt describes how he deals with criticism at his attempts to achieve something:

It is not the critic who counts;
not the man who points out how the strong man stumbles,
or where the doer of deeds could have done them better.
The credit belongs to the man who is actually in the arena,
whose face is marred by dust and sweat and blood;
who strives valiantly;
who errs,
comes up short again and again,
because there is no effort without error and shortcoming;
but who does actually strive to do the deeds;
who knows the great enthusiasms,
the great devotions; who spends himself in a worthy cause;
who at the best knows in the end
the triumph of high achievement,
and who at the worst, if he fails,
at least fails while daring greatly,
so that his place shall never be with those
cold and timid souls
who neither know victory nor defeat.

EXERCISE: improvising

How do you practice failing? Simply by doing it.

But there's another way, a kind of intermediate step that is incredibly fun to do, and useful at the same time.

"Improvisation Sport" became famous by Boom Chicago, an improvisational comedy group. It's not only for professionals. There are many amateur groups who take a lot of pleasure in practicing this theater sport. You can also follow courses and business trainings in this type of improvisation.

Improvising is based on five principles:
- Acting in the here and now
- Accepting a given situation by saying 'yes, and...' (instead of 'yes, but...')
- Seeking out danger
- Making the other person shine
- Daring to fail

One of the warming up exercises mostly revolves around that last principle.

It's simple. In the first round you walk through the room, pointing at items that you name out loud. 'Lamp', 'table', 'chair', 'ceiling' and so on.

During the second round you walk through the same room and again you point at items, but this time you call out completely different words. For example, 'apple pie', 'elephant', 'Eiffel Tower' and so on. Or you name a table a fridge and vice versa. It doesn't matter what you say, as long as it isn't the actual name of the object.

You'll notice that it is a very confusing concept. We're so trained to call things by their correct names that it takes effort to let this go.

Some people get used to it very quickly and have no trouble whatsoever with this exercise; they even have fun. Others completely get stuck and may even get a blackout.

By occasionally doing this simple, innocent exercise, you'll train yourself in letting go of fixed norms and you'll give your brains some leeway for thinking in different ways. Slowly but surely you'll get used to the idea that there is no right or wrong, and therefore you can't actually fail at all.

It is fun to do this exercise at home with friends or family, or at the office with clients or colleagues.

'It's risky to be safe.'

– Seth Godin –

'We don't do it because it is easy,

we do it because it is hard.'

– John F. Kennedy –

(on the eve of the first manned flight

to the moon)

Perseverance

Nobody said it would be easy. But if you don't persevere, you'll never know if you would have made it, after all. All success stories have an untold part: the part of the many failures that preceded the ultimate success.

So, you have to work hard to eventually get to where you want to be. But you can't always keep pushing yourself; take time to recharge your battery. And stop to see what you have already achieved instead of blindly staring at that distant goal. Also, involve the people who are helping you in these intermediate stops.

This part consists of the following chapters and interviews:

Celebrate and share your successes
Interview with Daphne and Frodo
Recharge your battery often
Interview with Johanna
Don't give up!
Interview with Nardy

Celebrate and share your successes

It's not about the destination; be sure to enjoy the journey.

If you have a big goal, the journey will probably take a while and it won't always be easy. Instead of looking at the long road that's ahead, filled with obstacles, I learned to occasionally stop and look at what I have already achieved. Look over your shoulder and enjoy the small steps you have made and the successes you have achieved. And as you probably achieved them with the help of others, be sure to share your successes with them. This way, everyone stays motivated and involved.

It's not only about the realization of dreams; it's also about enjoying the road there and the dreaming itself. 'It's a challenge to not only look ahead, but to also enjoy the small steps that you have taken today in the desired direction, as well as the new insights, the special encounters and the experiences that take place,' Hilda and Bas say after their Caribbean sailing trip and the start of their own business (page 46).

On YouTube there's a short video of a bunch of guys who thought up an absurd project. Afterwards, you'll see how they share their joy. The energy that is released is contagious! Check out 'waterslide – small pool' on YouTube.

Coins for Care was such a lengthy project (it cost years of preparation work followed by years of collecting and processing all the coins) that it was difficult to keep everyone motivated and involved. In addition, there were so many parties involved that it was, unfortunately, impossible to stay in personal contact with everyone. Therefore, once in a while I'd sent out a newsletter to all charities, volunteers, sponsors and participating stores. Initially it was intended to answer frequently asked questions, so it would save me time. But everyone seemed to really appreciate the newsflashes. I tried to motivate the charities to begin additional collections amongst their donors in order to stimulate a bit of competition. When I'd share how successful a collection had been, other charities were motivated to organize something, too.

For the volunteers I collected fun tidbits and anecdotes, such as the story of a wedding ring and a love letter that were found in a collection box. I also asked them to share their own experiences, so we could share them, in turn, with others. This way, a constant stream of information and motivation kept flowing between all parties.

We sent sponsors and participating stores extra PR updates, with overviews of all media attention, clippings from newspapers and magazines, and television and radio appearances. I always tried to name a few sponsors in interviews, so they knew that I greatly valued their help. Moreover, a lot of publicity helped the person who had agreed to sponsoring in the name of a company to justify this internally.

Nowadays this could be easily done by using the social media. But back then everything went by me and had to be targeted and emailed to a specific group. Because I had to write this newsletter and PR update, I was constantly searching for fun stories and positive news. This helped me to shift my attention from things that did not run smoothly...

In his books, Sir Richard Branson describes how he created his successful Virgin Empire. As a sixteen-year-old he already published a magazine for students. Then he set up a mail-order firm for records, and later the Virgin record label. When his businesses (the music stores, the airline and many of his 360(!) companies) became successful, he gave yearly three-day feasts for all those involved. Sometimes there were even sixty thousand invitees. Richard insisted on greeting everyone personally at the door and shaking their hands. This may have caused him RSI by the end of the three days, but at least he would have personally thanked everyone for their contribution to Virgin's success. He even attributes this as one of his success factors.

For years, Nelleke Griffioen worked as a communication consultant and then started up her own PassionPractice, where she guided people in following their hearts and passion. She organized all sorts of fun gatherings and sent out frequent newsletters with inspiring stories and stimulating tips. This way, she built a large network of people who want to live more from their hearts. Meanwhile, toge-

ther with her husband and their two children, the family follows their common passion: the mountains. As they always spent their holidays in the mountains, they decided to move to Austria in 2009, where they now run a mountain refuge, called De Berghut. A place surrounded by mountains where people can experience nature and meet and inspire each other. By means of her cheerful newsletters from their mountain resort, her 'followers' are stimulated to think about their own dreams. Moreover, this way Nelleke lets her readers know that they can rent a room there for inspiration, development and holiday. A magnificent combination.
www.deberghut.com

With the latest technology and social media it is very easy to stay in touch with the people around you.
An increasing number of people who set out to travel keep people at home up-to-date using their own website or special blogging sites such as: http://whereareyou.net.

Personally I have been an enthusiastic Twitter-user for about two years now. The fun thing about it is that you'll never overload anyone with unwanted messages. Everyone decides for themselves who they follow and what they do and do not want to hear. Recently, in a bar in Amsterdam, I ran into two former fellow students. They had been a few years above me at Nyenrode University, so we had never had a lot of contact. Yet, one of them said, to my surprise, 'Esther, I thoroughly enjoy your adventures; I follow all your posts!' Subsequently we started talking and he told me, among other things, about an extreme expedition to Antarctica he had recently done. By chance, I had already heard about this from the 'tweets' of a common friend who had joined him. And so we came to the conclusion that it's a small world when you can learn so much about people you only vaguely know. However, it can be incredibly inspiring!
And of course it doesn't all have to be digital or reach the masses. An 'old-fashioned' phone call, a flower or a thank-you card is also much valued.

Together with PriceWaterhouseCoopers (PWC) I organized, through the Donor Organization, the yearly Transparency Prize for the most transparent annual charity report. Each summer, PWC would work for months on this, as a whole team of accountants systematically analyzed and classified the hundreds of submitted annual reports. The teeny-weeny Donor Organization could hardly contribute to this. Neither in manpower nor in money. Yet I did want to show some moral support to PWC and let them know that we greatly valued their effort. At some point, together with my interns I got the idea to have a huge cream cake delivered at PWC. So all the accountants working on the project could have a slice. It wasn't much more expensive to have the logo of the Transparency Prize printed onto the cake. This gesture cost very little and it made a lot of hardworking people happy. By doing these kinds of small things we tried to keep an otherwise impossible partnership going.

When I visited other sponsors of the Donor Organization (often large businesses or banks), I got into the habit of bringing some treats during coffee breaks. A bag of pastries from the bakery or something else that they wouldn't normally have at the office. These people often worked on my projects in their spare time, without being paid for it, so the interaction had to be pleasant. Hence the festive touch with the coffee. I noticed from the jokes that were made about this that the gesture was appreciated.

exercise

EXERCISE:

Which people in your life are involved with your dream? Who 'profits' from it, who works on it? Who is interested in staying up-to-date?

Think of five fun, playful ways to keep these parties up-to-date and thank them.

From now on, make a habit of showing your appreciation and sharing progress each time you see or email such a person.

Your attitude
makes the difference
between a nightmare
and an adventure.

Young doctors Daphne (31) and Frodo (33) drove their Land Rover from Amsterdam to Cape Town and worked in hospitals along the way and at their destination.

We wanted to make a beautiful trip and do something charitable along the way. As students we had traveled through Australia and New Zealand for a few months, and we enjoyed campervans as a mode of transportation. You take your home along with you and you're very close to nature. You're in charge of your direction and you can visit places where buses don't go. This gave us the idea to travel by car. Frodo's stepbrother sold us his Land Cruiser. Since Frodo had done an internship in Cape Town, we chose that as our destination. And the trip from the Netherlands to South Africa is the longest overland journey you can make in Africa: the adventure appealed to us.

After we received our degrees in Medicine, we first worked for a year. Daphne wanted to specialize in Tropical Medicine and Frodo wanted to become a plastic surgeon. We contacted hospitals in Cape Town as well as countries that were on our way. We came up with a catchy name for our project: *Driving Doctors*.
We wanted to help in local hospitals, hand out medical supplies and at the same time get a feel for the state of foreign medical aid. All those non-governmental organizations (NGO) have people driving around in large, expensive Jeeps; how valuable is that? We also wanted to find a project along the way to which we could donate money and medical supplies. Many of our friends wanted to help charities, but they did not know how. They were keen to support us if we managed to find a good project. A Dutch hospital donated their excess sterile materials for us to distribute in African hospitals.
We approached the media. Our story, a young doctor couple hea-ding out to travel through Africa for a charitable cause, became hugely popular. It all happened so fast, there was no way to contain media attention. They even called us for an interview while we were on the ferry to Sudan!
We prepared for the trip with an open mind. Whether the car would be in good shape or not, whether we would get loads or very few

supplies for local hospitals, we would go anyway. It didn't have to be perfect for us.

Friends and family were very concerned, however. 'You have to think of your careers. Wouldn't it be better if you focused on specializing?' We received many well-meant warnings and pieces of advice: We had to bring no less than twenty gallons of water. We couldn't drive through the north of Kenya without a military convoy; we could be kidnapped and what not. Dutch mentality is not really focused on doing things that are different. This was often disheartening for us. It took us a lot of effort to stick to our plan.

The higher your expectations, the more setbacks you will experience. We actually didn't have any expectations; we simply went! Considering all the negative messages and warnings we received, the trip was actually a piece of cake. We enjoyed the various countries we visited, the people we met, nature's magnificence and each other. It is actually very special to experience something like this together. Of course things went wrong, now and then. But everything always worked out, in the end.

For example, the car broke down twice and we had to stay in the same place for a while until it was fixed. This way, you have a lot more contact with locals than as a tourist. In Ethiopia we stranded in a tiny village where everyone still used horse carts. The only car in the village was ours and it had broken down... Yet, eventually, they did succeed in repairing it. In Sudan's capital, Khartoum, we were

overwhelmed by the hospitality of the people. A guy called Aladdin insisted that we would sleep over in his house. For the duration of one week we experienced him and his family up close. We managed to turn a misfortune into a gift. For example, during the forced delay we decided to talk to a traditional medicine man; something we would have otherwise never done.

We have also been very lucky and we have learned to rely on this a little. For example, before we departed we were advised to travel by convoy because of rebels. However, this meant you had to offer a ride to a soldier and we had no space in our car. So we had to drive the road ourselves. The road was terrible, with many potholes and stones. We continually had flat tires. At some point the tires were so done for that they could no longer be repaired. One of us had to stay with the car and the other would set out to get help in the village three hours down the road. It was quite stressful because dusk was setting in. Daphne accepted a ride on the roof of a truck. An hour later the truck also got a flat tire. Thankfully another truck passed and she was welcome to hitch a ride. 'Will I ever see Frodo again?' she wondered, scared and lonely.

Meanwhile, Frodo waited with the car and made coffee on a fire. There was not much else to do. Then a dignitary in military clothes passed in an expensive car with military escort. They had no fewer than four spare tires, of which two somewhat fitted on our car. They insisted that one of the soldiers would travel with Frodo while he searched for Daphne. It was really a very dangerous region. When Frodo reached the first truck, still parked by the road, and he did not see Daphne, he got quite worried. Thanks to hands-and-feet communication he understood that she was in the next truck, and this way they found each other again.

In the evening, when we arrived at the village where we had wanted to seek help, everyone there seemed to be drunk and the atmosphere was aggressive. It was a good thing the dignitary had passed by, because if Daphne had arrived in this village by herself...

Using our website, we kept our friends, family and sponsors informed of our adventures. All the stories that we placed are, in hindsight, also beautiful memories for ourselves.

Along the way we helped out in local hospitals and handed out the medical supplies that we had brought. We stayed a bit longer in Malawi, where we heard about a project that we wanted to support. The mission hospital there had started an outreach clinic, from where nurses frequently visited remote villages. For many people there, walking to the hospital would take several days, which was frequently too far. When a nurse arrived, patients from various villages would gather in one single village. Pregnant women and other patients could then be examined, babies would be vaccinated, and so on. A fantastic project. In one of the villages, a small building had to be built, from where the outreach clinic could do its work. We helped finance this. It wasn't a 'white doctor' project; it was a project of the people. Everyone helped building and maintaining the clinic. A real community project.

It is difficult to assess if this kind of aid is useful. There are so many factors that you can't foresee. For example, the otherwise great outreach project also had an unintended side effect. The mission hospital started so many initiatives that everyone wanted to work there. As a consequence, the other hospital in the region, a state hospital, had trouble finding and keeping enough good staff.

Because of all the publicity surrounding our trip, apparently there were expectations that our trip was more focused on charity than on some fun traveling. Consequently, sometimes we were criticized. For us it was exactly the other way around. We wanted to travel in a fun way, and contribute something in the process. We certainly succeeded at this. We also sparked some discussion on the use of foreign medical aid.

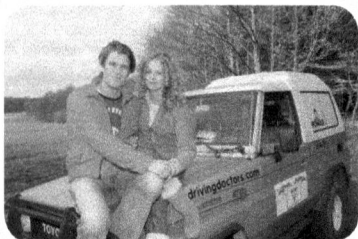

Tips from Daphne and Frodo:

Don't make your dream too rigid; try not to limit yourself; don't try to do too much.

Don't let fears or negative stories lead you. Do listen to advice and take from it what you think you could use.

If you don't expect too much, you won't be disappointed. Take it as it comes; experience the positive.

Try not to stay in control; let yourself be carried away.

Just do it!

Recharge your battery often

Where do you get your energy and motivation?

You can't always keep your bow drawn. If you want to shoot better, you'll sometimes have to let go of the tension on your bow, and build it again.

What's important is that you can let things go once in a while. Have you ever experienced being very busy with a project and something just doesn't work? At some point, highly frustrated, you'll head home. You'll keep trying to find a solution. And then, when you're having a shower, walking your dog or reading a book, and you're not thinking about it at all, suddenly you know what you must do! You can also purposely create these moments of inspiration. At successful innovative companies such as 3M and Google, employees are required to spend a percentage of their time on other things. Playing golf or computer games, reading comics and so on. This stimulates creativity.

To me, what's important is variety. I know that I am on a roll when I'm in the Netherlands for a few of weeks, and I can join the 'rat race', giving workshops and talks; I can drive all over the country, see friends, do things and so on. I can keep up this high pace for a short while, because I know that I have reserved a period of rest in Curaçao or somewhere else. After a while at such a peaceful location, I will have managed to digest all the information and ideas in my head, and then I'll feel a need for the high-paced life again; then I'll return to 'civilization'. I have found the ideal combination for me, and this gives me a lot of strength and peace of mind.

Artist Michaelangelo (page 190) knows how to put his personal process into words quite aptly: 'When I move within the world, I can clearly see my inner silence. When I stay in the same, comfortable place, my worldly thoughts are in motion and my environment is still.'

My peace and inspiration comes from travelling (preferably without a plan), and being completely in the moment. This is what I experienced in that cave in Malaysia where I was 'hidden' for two weeks for the European version of the reality show Survivor. In Curaçao I swim half a mile every day. The rhythm and the fish that I meet along the way give me peace and inspiration. I have had some of my best ideas and solved so many problems while swimming! While my thoughts are completely somewhere else, a good idea may simply surface. In the cooler European countries I also get energy from walking in nature and sleeping enough. Other people get energy from going out, dancing or sports, or they swear by yoga or meditation.

Nardy (page 246) ordered her mind while on her pilgrimage to Santiago de Compostela.

Maanwilla (page 162) recharges her battery by leafing through cookbooks and preparing delicious meals. 'It costs me a lot of energy to do too much at once. I solve this by seeking peace in everyday things. For example, by paying attention while I dress myself. I notice that this determines how you feel that day. Or, for example, by reading the newspaper with a nice cup of jasmine tea. Or, when cycling, and consciously feeling the wind through my hair. I can do this every day; I am not dependent on external circumstances or on other people.'

Sylvia (page 62) advises to occasionally seek out silence, through nature, meditation or yoga, so you can 'hear' your own heart.

Determine for yourself: what gives me energy? What gives me peace? However busy you are, plan these moments or activities into your day. Especially in busy periods, when you might sooner be inclined to skip your hour of exercise. Plan time in your busy schedule for your 'recharging activity'. This is just as important as all those other urgent things you must do; maybe even more important...

'Grant me the serenity to accept the things I cannot change, the courage to change the things I can, and the wisdom to know the difference.'

If you don't sow, you'll know for sure nothing will grow and you will never reap.

If you do sow, you will have a limited influence on the result. If you choose a good spot with enough sun, if you provide good seeds and good soil, till the earth well, frequently provide water and take good care of the land, then you know that you have optimized all the circumstances that you can influence. The rest you must leave to nature.

It's the same with dreams. Do what you can to prepare: sow and optimize all circumstances that you can influence. And then let it go. If it still doesn't work, then it just wasn't meant to be or it wasn't the right moment. You can still decide to try again, in a different way, in another place, or at another moment, or to pursue a different dream. At least you can't blame yourself for not having tried.

Johanna (31) wanted to combine development aid in Africa with work in the Swiss business sector. When no charity accepted her as a volunteer, she decided to initiate her own project in Ethiopia. Afterwards she moved to Geneva on the off chance. At a relatively young age she learned to let go all certainties and choose her own path. She now combines her job with 'charity' close to home, by helping people who are less fortunate.

After my bachelor's degree in General Social Studies and my master's in *Conflict Studies and Human Rights*, I wanted to work in development aid. I had enjoyed an excellent education and now wanted to discover to what extent I could make a real contribution to the world. But without any work experience in that field, the search proved to be difficult. I wasn't accepted anywhere. Both large and smaller development aid organizations said, 'no work experience? No job for you.' They wanted someone with at least two years of work experience, even for volunteer work! I found it unreasonable. How to ever get experience if nobody offers you the opportunity?

I therefore decided to find a project myself. A friend of a friend had established an orphanage in Ethiopia and he welcomed me to conduct a performance evaluation and support their cause. It was a perfect and valuable opportunity. I loved to be among the children. The project wasn't easy though, being the only Western person, but it was eye opening and educative. Being there, I realized that the development of a country's business sector is crucial to a country's development and sustainability. The charity project was an enriching experience, but I decided to use my knowledge and skills in the business sector instead. I found I could add more value by helping from this position for example through fundraising and direct support.

Geneva had always drawn me, although I had never been there. When I was twenty-six and had just returned from Ethiopia, I thought: job or no job, I'm just going to Geneva. It is much harder to apply for jobs from a distance. At least when you're there you can connect with people. It also shows potential employers that you're really serious about getting a job and living there. I estimated that I would, without any financial support, be able to pay my bills for four months. 'If I don't manage to find a job, it won't be the end of the world; I'll simply return back home,' I told myself. My friends and family supported me, but they secretly thought: you'll never manage. I am someone who always wants to stay in control; now I had lost all my security at once. And strangely enough this gave me peace. I surrendered to it; I prayed a lot and I had faith. Within a month I had a job at a bank! I'd never thought I'd end up there, but I thoroughly enjoyed myself. I learned a lot and I had fun colleagues. I very much enjoyed living and working in Geneva, a vibrant environment where it was easy to make new friends within the international and local community. In addition: the General Director had seen my CV and asked if I wanted to help the bank with their charity foundation. My dreams seemed to come true at last.

But in October 2008, the financial crisis began. At this time, my father worked for another bank and he did well for his clients. Nonetheless he was dismissed, because his vision did not correspond with the bank's ideas.

Instead of feeling down and rejected, he called me and said, 'Johanna, I want you to be my business partner!' What?! I was going through a difficult period myself at the bank, but to work together with my father? I would have never, ever foreseen this. However, I considered it a challenge that I did not want to miss out on. Even if it meant that I would have to step out of my comfort zone again, move to a different city and rebuild a private and business life in another new environment.

It also meant taking new risks. When you start your own business from scratch, it can either succeed or fail. However, we felt very much supported by our faith. And it was a plus that I had had a good education; I knew exactly how to help my father. If he would have had to train me first, I don't think we would have succeeded.

Right now we're three years down the road since my father and I started working as partners and independent consultants. It wasn't easy to start in the beginning, but we are blessed and we had already achieved our goal for the first year well ahead of schedule. We are a strong and enormously motivated team. We grew closer to each other. My father and I are partners who can be fully open and honest to each other. We want the best for both of us, which creates an encouraging, dynamic and respectful environment. I had never thought that it could be so much fun working together with my father.

Meanwhile, the time had come to make a link to development aid, not only in Africa, but also in my close environment. Especially in the West there is a lot of need for help and support, because everyone lives in their own separate world. Therefore, I try to support the young and elderly in my direct surroundings. This has been partially made possible through my church, which has many ministries where you can use your talents. For example, I've organized sports events, activities with teen girls from poor families and meetings for business people. But I also learned another important lesson: to invest in myself... And at the moment I did so I got to know my husband whom I married only a year later.

I have found a beautiful balance. I used to think that I could only really help in Africa, but I learned that your purpose doesn't always have to be far from home. You're also very important to the people around you. This means being there for your friends and family and taking time for them.

Even though I live in Switzerland, I still have good contact with my friends in the Netherlands. We stay in touch by phone and email and I try to visit them when I am in the Netherlands. Additionally, each year three friends come to Switzerland to visit me. This all has shown me that you don't have to see each other every day in order to have a good relationship. You don't lose real friends; they'll always support you. Don't let the geographic distance to your friends hinder you to make a choice, or take on a challenge. Taking on a challenge may actually strengthen your friendship; you'll notice who your real friends are. In a relationship it's easy to love each other when life is a bed of roses. Only when the going gets tough, you'll know if you really love one another. Then you must invest in the relationship and you'll grow together. It's the same with friendship.

If you have a vision, you want to follow your dreams, and so you'll head in a certain direction. But you can't look into the future and you won't know what is best for you, in the end. I used to always want to be a vet. I ended up in a completely different sector, but it feels good and I am content with my life. I feel guided. It is very special, very beautiful. It's not all about performing or proving yourself. You are not what you have achieved, you are the person who you are and the qualities that you already have without proving them first. Knowing this provides a real sense of peace which helps me face challenges. If you don't follow your dreams, you'll never know if you would have succeeded. This would have made me feel restless. I have now seen all sides; this is how it should have been.

It's also the way I met my husband. First when I had let go and let God be in control and guide me, I was able to meet "the husband of my dreams". I actually exactly knew what kind of man I was looking for, but first realized this when I met him: He's the one! And I followed my dream... A year later we had two amazing wedding days in both the Netherlands and Switzerland, like a fairytale, but on our flight back from honeymoon I got ill for months. I had expected to have another start from marriage and on top of that I didn't have time for being ill businesswise, but apparently I again had to learn a lesson: that my husband loves me just the way I am and not because of how fit I am or by what I have achieved. It also showed me that you can follow your dream, or actually, you have to follow your dream, but not because you think that otherwise you're not the beautiful, talented and loving person you'd like to be as you already àre this person! Instead, you should follow your dream as God has given you the capability and talents to do so, in order to use them for helping others ànd yourself and for fully enjoying your life.

My friends and family have supported me. This really has made a difference. The first time you leave behind all certainties and your familiar environment, is the hardest. But I've noticed that it's easy to meet new people with the right attitude knowing that you're worth it... The next time you won't feel so alone. It's a matter of giving and taking. However, I've also noticed that with the right attitude, you'll be able to follow the core of your dream: no matter what!

Tips from Johanna:

I have learned that you can't plan your dream and it is not within your own hands, but you can 'receive' it if you're open to it. Don't get discouraged by the situation in which you find yourself that tend to be difficult; have faith that God gave you certain talents and a purpose in your life, also to go after your dream. However, don't focus too much on your dream and allow yourself to be flexible. You'll see that your dream will, one way or another, sooner or later, comes true.

It doesn't matter where you are; what matters is how you deal with your dream. Because I carried this dream within me, doors opened and possibilities arose. The next step was to take on these possibilities and put my heart in it. And I have done this, thankfully, even though the future became uncertain and I had to step out of my safe environment.

I have learned that you are 'prepared' for your dream, or for that which you carry in your heart. This also includes obstacles.

Think, when you take on the challenge: what is the worst that can happen? What can I win and what can I lose if I do this? Put it in writing.

If you make a choice, you must go for it; don't keep doubting. Just do it. Do what you can and then surrender. You must give the best of you, and that is all you can do; you will at least have tried.

Give yourself a deadline. Think relatively: what are a few months in the perspective of a whole life?

Don't do it half-heartedly or from a distance; be sure to be present on the spot.

When you fall, you'll learn how to get up.

A beautiful passage from the Bible that gave and gives me a lot of support is: 1 Corinthians 10:13 – 'No temptation has overtaken you except what is common to mankind. And God is faithful; he will not let you be tempted beyond what you can bear. But when you are tempted, he will also provide a way out so that you can endure it.'

If you really want something, there's always a way to get there. Give yourself that chance, have faith, go for it.

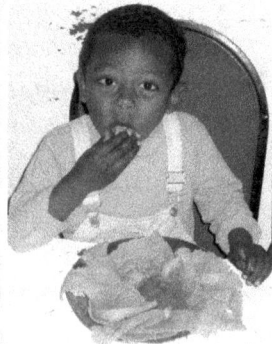

'Tough times never last, but tough people do!"

240

Don't give up!

Don't get demotivated if things don't go as planned. Things always turn out different than you expected; be flexible and make the best of it. Setbacks will make you stronger. Keep having faith in your dream!

Sylvester Stallone wanted to become an actor and auditioned many times. Yet he was rejected everywhere. Because he failed to succeed, he started writing movie scripts. At an audition (where he was, once again, rejected), he met producers who saw potential in his movie script about a boxer called Rocky. They wanted a famous actor to play the lead. However, Sylvester insisted that he would play the lead himself. Initially, they offered him 25,000 dollars for the script. They kept increasing their offer up to 333,000 dollars! Sylvester refused. He did not want to sell the script separately; he wanted to play the lead!

In the end, the producers gave way, but because Sylvester wasn't a famous actor, the film budget was much smaller. That's why they had to improvise a lot, for example when running up the famous staircase of the Art Museum in Philadelphia. They did this without any formal permission. Early in the morning, they snuck out of a van like thieves; Sylvester did his famous scene on the staircase and everything was filmed with a hand-held camera.

What happened next is known to everybody. Sylvester became famous as Rocky, he earned a lot of money with it and inspired millions of people. What if he had given up? If he had stopped wanting to audition after all those rejections? If he had not continued writing his scripts? If he had given in and let another person play the lead? If he had not continued to work out and lost his faith and his convictions?

'Many of life's failures are people who did not realize how close they were to success when they gave up.'

– Thomas Edison –

There are many more stories about famous people or products of which we would have never heard if they had given up.
A mother on welfare had written a book. She couldn't find a publisher who wanted to publish her story about a young schoolboy wizard. Despite the many setbacks in her life and the many rejections of her manuscript, she stayed positive and persevered. Finally she found a publisher, Bloomsbury, prepared to publish her book. Now J. K. Rowling is the most successful (living) author worldwide, thanks to her Harry Potter books.

The same goes for the book *Chicken Soup for the Soul*, which has sold more than one hundred million copies worldwide in 54 languages; this book too, initially had trouble finding a publisher. Motivational speakers Jack Canfield and Mark Victor Hansen inexhaustibly lugged their book from publisher to publisher. Finally they were lucky and their book with short, inspirational stories was published. It became a bestseller!

Oprah Winfrey had a terrible childhood. In stead of love, there was abuse, poverty and much misery. When, one day, she saw *The Supremes* sing on television, a new world opened up for her. Black women on television? She would have never thought that possible. She had never had a role model. Now she thought: this is how I want to be. Oprah then worked really hard and suffered many setbacks in order to get closer to her goal, step by step. In spite of her terrible youth, or perhaps because of it, Oprah now has a career as the most well known talk show host in the world.

Henri Peteri was involved with the launch of instant soup in 1970. He thought it strange that if you wanted to make a bowl of soup in 30 seconds, you first had to wait five minutes for the kettle to boil.

There must be a way to get boiling water directly from the tap. Henri quit his job and spent years messing around in his cellar until he had developed the first prototype.

Users were madly enthusiastic, but the general opinion in the kitchen industry was that such a device was 'not necessary'. Henri considered that they had also said such a thing once about vacuum cleaners, and now nobody can do without. He persevered. He developed much better models of his Quooker, but at some point his money had come to and end. He had taken no less than seven(!) mortgages on his house.

Things got going only in 1985, when his son Niels came to help in the business. In 1992 the first Quookers were brought into production and only in 2000 did they reach a turning point: for the first time they made a profit.

Now Quooker has become known internationally in designer kitchens. The Peteris have worked hard for it for over thirty years, but finally they succeeded. If this isn't a persistent family! Their complete story can be read at www.quooker.com.

**'Do not lose hold of your dreams
or aspirations.
For if you do, you may still exist,
but you will have ceased to live.'**

– Thoreau –

In his book Outliers: *The Story of Success*, Malcolm Gladwell states that you should have at least ten thousand hours of experience before you will be successful at something. For example, The Beatles spent weeks playing eight hours a day for a pittance in small bars in Germany before they became so good that they had a definite breakthrough. Malcolm studied the success of sportspeople, lawyers and pianists, and divulges that the secret of their success is almost always based on the ten-thousand-hour rule.

The famous author and researcher also shares examples of cultural notions about hard work. Asians, for example, have a very different understanding of persistence, perseverance and hard work than Europeans have. This is probably because of their agricultural society. In order to grow rice you must work three times harder than if you grow grains. This hard work and perseverance is part of Asian culture, and it can be quite useful, for example, during math lessons. According to Gladwell, this is the reason that Japanese, Chinese and South Korean children score much higher on math exams than their western peers.

'Victory belongs to the most persevering.'

– Napoleon Bonaparte –

Whatever you want to achieve, don't be afraid to work hard for it, keep on trying, keep practicing until you perfect your 'thing' and above all: keep having faith!

'A man is not finished when

he's defeated;

he's finished when

he quits...'

– Richard Nixon –

Nardy (39) wants to have a child, but she does not want to be a fulltime mother. John and Eric are a happily married gay couple who really want a child. The three of them decide to take on the adventure, but things do not go as easily as planned.

I'm not really the motherly type. I like children, but I'm very attached to my freedom and independence. I travel a lot, I have my own business and I find time to myself important. But last year I thought: I'm thirty-eight and if I ever want children, I should start to think about it now.

My relationship had just ended. I had also had a burnout and I was unable to take much. Lovesick and confused, I decided to walk nine hundred kilometers to Santiago de Compostela to put my life in order. This was very good for me. I got back to my old self completely. While walking, life became simple and manageable and I thought about what I wanted:

- expand my business. I had literally thought it out step-by-step;
- children;
- a great partner.

You can't force the latter, but I could work with the first two. I admire women who succeed at raising a child by themselves, but I would only dare to enter motherhood with a good partner. So far, all my relationships have not lasted more than two years. So in order to be able to offer a child a stable basis, I wanted to be in a relationship for at least two years with a man who would be, in my eyes, an excellent father. I had just left a failed relationship and I had to admit that chances for those perfect circumstances wouldn't be so high in the coming years.

I did not envision myself to be a good single mother. However, I knew a fantastic gay couple and I realized that with them I would dare to take on the challenge. I talked to them about it and they thought it was very special that I suggested it, but they weren't ready for children.

The idea of getting a child together with a gay couple stayed on my mind. It appealed to me because the child would have a warm family situation, and I could play a part in the background, without getting into a conflict with an adoptive mother. I am afraid that I might quarrel with another woman about the child's upbringing, or that she might feel threatened by me. This could be a confusing situation for the child.

A friend pointed me to a Dutch website where many gay couples with a desire to have children get in touch with each other.

I placed a personal ad:

I was so overwhelmed by fun reactions that I removed my ad two weeks later. I intuitively picked three couples. These people had in

Hi, I'd like to introduce myself: my name is Nardy and I want to be a mother. I am an entrepreneur, I work in IT, I studied law, I am internationally oriented, and I have a friendly, open, and liberal character. My life mostly takes place between work, traveling, friends and family, and between Curaçao, Amsterdam and a bit of South America (through a project). I am looking for the most fantastic gay couple in the world that wants to have a child with me. Think of spontaneous, pleasant, open, happy, and preferably university-educated people who want to be parents and play a prominent part in the child's upbringing. I want to have a bond with the child but a role in the background. I'm open to discussing what your and my roles will look like; I'm flexible and all facets can be talked about. I do have one 'hard' condition: the interests of the future child must take first place. Do you share these ideas and does this notion appeal to you, too? Then let's enjoy meeting each other in a relaxed environment. I'm looking forward to your reactions!

common that they did not tell a 'politically correct' story, they did not pretend to be more than they were, and they were simply themselves and content with their lives. The reactions that stood out to me were from two Dutch couples and a couple from Kenya. Well, geography was not a factor; this became clear to my environment soon enough.

Together with two female friends I organized introductory dinners at my house. The first Dutch couple was a lot of fun, but they turned out to be in an orientation phase. They were therefore not suitable; I didn't have time for that... I wanted to get straight to action! The second Dutch couple were really great. They were instantly my first choice. I would have taken the decision right there and then, but the couple from Kenya was to come to Amsterdam especially for our meeting. They were Dutch, but they ran an orphanage and a school in Kenya and they had also set up a few lodges in order to finance their projects.

John arrived first; he wanted to follow my footsteps and also walk Santiago. Eric had to stay behind in Kenya in order to run everything there. I instantly fell for John! He was exactly how he had seemed in his emails and on the phone, and so lovable, huggable, and I knew: with you I can take on the world! Eric arrived a bit later and he, too, was everything I had hoped for. Such a delicious couple, too.

The three of us walked the last 100 miles to Santiago de Compostela together, so we could get to know each other better along the way. During our hikes we discussed everything at great length. The idea is that John will become the natural father and Eric will acknowledge the child as his before birth; the child will also get his last name. This way, they're both the child's real father. John and Eric will move in with me just before birth. The first year they will take the child with them to Kenya. There they want to transfer the management of their project to the right people. A huge picture of mommy will hang in the house. The tickets are fixed, as well as visiting arrangements for the grandmothers and grandfathers. As soon as the child begins to talk, they'll move to Amsterdam. It would be too dangerous in Kenya, where homosexuality is not accepted (expect a prison sentence of 14 years). Imagine the child would start talking about his two daddies!

We set up a 'communication plan' for within the family, we found a lawyer and a notary with lots of experience in these kinds of cases and we made an extensive parenting plan. I will even pay a maintenance allowance. Down to the last detail we discussed what we would do should I hesitate to give them the child in the end; I can't imagine this to be the case, because I wholeheartedly love the idea. John and Eric have been together for eleven years and I have complete faith in them. And to my great surprise they proposed to each other at the end of the Pilgrim's Mass in Santiago de Compostela!

We had thought about every scenario, except one: what if I would get into a relationship in the meanwhile? And this is exactly what happened. I fell in love with Jan, whom I had known for years and who temporarily stayed in my house. As he was one of my closer friends, he knew everything about our 'project' and he supported us. But now it did become extra complicated. What if our relationship would last and we would want a child for ourselves?

As this is not really applicable yet, we'll see what we'll do when the time comes. Jan believes, just as I do, that we should be together for at least two years before we can think about children. An advantage for Jan and me: if we ever want children for ourselves, all the 'preparatory work' has been done. But of course it is a strange situation, and it can be quite tricky for him: how to explain this to people around you?

Anyway, the communication plan for family and friends succeeded and we got a lot of support from our immediate surroundings. When everything was settled, we started with the IVF. This was quite a difficult period, because things didn't go as expected. As I had had two ectopic pregnancies in a distant past, I don't have any Fallopian

tubes anymore, and I needed help getting pregnant. But the gynecologist who knew my situation and had promised to help me committed suicide! I had to recover from this; it had impacted me deeply.

After this, I started approaching hospitals to ask for help with our 'project', as I started calling it. A few hospitals rejected me with an excuse; others were more open about why they didn't want to cooperate. Apparently it is not accepted in the Netherlands if you want to conceive a child together with or for a gay couple. It is viewed as an unusual situation, in which psychological support must be given.

Eventually John and I went for a consultation in a certain hospital. We didn't really go into our private situation and they didn't really ask about it, either. The doctor even said to an intern, 'look, they're living at the same address; you should always check this.' They also asked how long we had known each other, which we answered truthfully: two years. I had become quite close with John anyway; we were holding hands and during the somewhat scary consultation in the hospital we automatically sought support from each other. So nobody asked about the 'unusual situation' and we could get started! Unfortunately the first attempt failed. Two weeks later I had a miscarriage.

Just before the second attempt, something happened that nobody could have foreseen. I was waiting for John and Eric at the airport when suddenly a camera team appeared. The presenter of the Dutch television program *Hello Goodbye,* asked whom I was waiting for. Enthusiastically, I blurted out that I was waiting for my 'bio-daddies'. The camera team looked at me, wide-eyed, and I cheerfully told them who John and Eric were and what we were going to do. I didn't quite stop to think that this would also be broadcast. Or that it might be seen by an employee of the lab in charge of the ovary work for our hospital. And then it turned out that the lab was Christian... and principally against gay parenting. Moreover, they interpreted our story as that we hadn't told the whole truth...

We were accused of fraud and the head of the IVF department threatened to destroy our leftover embryos. I was instantly furious. 'Don't touch my children!' I cried, completely worked up because of the strong hormones. John and Eric jumped in and explained everything in a beautiful letter to the lab and hospital. The latter turned out to be very understanding and cooperative, but their collaboration with the lab was at stake. After many discussions we came to an acceptable compromise. The existing embryos would be transferred, but no third attempt would be made by them.

Thankfully, the hospital referred us to a medical center where sexual preference is not an issue so we could continue the IVF treatment. The center considers help with fertility problems as a medical affair and they'll help any woman who wants a child, regardless of the family constitution.

Meanwhile, however, another problem occurred. All the hormones had not only made me gain 30 pounds in five months; I also increasingly had belly aches. At some point I could no longer sit, lie down or walk. It turned out I had a uterine fibroid, which had to be surgically removed. This was quite an impact; therefore we have now taken a time-out.

For a third attempt we're welcome in the medical center, but I'm not looking forward to the hormones. They are extremely strong and I find it a physical challenge. John and Eric have been great, but we do find it increasingly difficult considering everything that has happened over the past time. Moreover, Jan is also not keen to go through more misery; I'm afraid he feels a little left out. Even John and Eric find the situation with the four of us a little uncomfortable, now, even though the three men really like each other.

Yet, I'm not prepared to give up. I'm simply looking for another option without hormones. And it turns out to exist! It's called IVM (in vitro maturation) and it is only done in the UK, in Canada, in Sweden and in Norway. There was an experiment in the Netherlands, too, but this turned out to be for women between the ages of 32 and 38. I am just one year too old. And so it is that IVM abroad will be our next adventure. And, of course, negotiations with my health insurance company.

Together, Jan, John, Eric and I, we have decided to wait until I am completely recovered from my surgery, and wait until the summer is over. I would personally like to try Sweden or Denmark. We could go there for a few days each month for an embryo transfer. Yes, it will be a very international child.

Of course I sometimes have my doubts. Am I taking Jan's feelings enough into account? I have also not forgotten the belly aches and the surgery. And those 30 extra pounds were quite a horror. But then, when I look into the eyes of John and Eric, I know why I am doing this, and any trace of doubt is erased. These are really the best fathers in the world I could have wished for our child.

Would I not have done it if I had known what kind of things I would encounter? No, I would have done it anyhow. This is what I want; the obstacles have only made me more convinced of this. A sportsman also makes sacrifices. You have a goal in mind and you go for it! And if it doesn't work, it doesn't work, but then at least you will have tried.

John and Eric still work in Kenya. Their real names have not been used for their safety.

'All our dreams can come true,

if we have the courage

to pursue them.'

– Walt Disney –

The Spiral of Creation

'The Spiral of Creation describes the natural path from wish to reality.'

When this book was almost finished, someone pointed me to the Spiral of Creation by Marinus Knoope. I was pleasantly surprised to see my own experiences and those of many interviewees portrayed so clearly. It can be clarifying to read through the steps of the Spiral of Creation, so you will recognize them when you come across them in practice. I hereby want to thank Marinus wholeheartedly for his great work and his permission to publish this information.

In the same way that spring blossoms foretell summer fruits, the wishes and desires of people foretell that which they may later realize. In the same way that fruit trees have exactly the qualities that make them capable of creating their own type of fruit, human beings have exactly the qualities that make them capable of realizing their own wishes and desires. In the same way that nature has a fixed route from blossom to fruit and from seed to harvest, nature also has a specific route from wish to reality. Marinus Knoope describes this route in twelve steps:

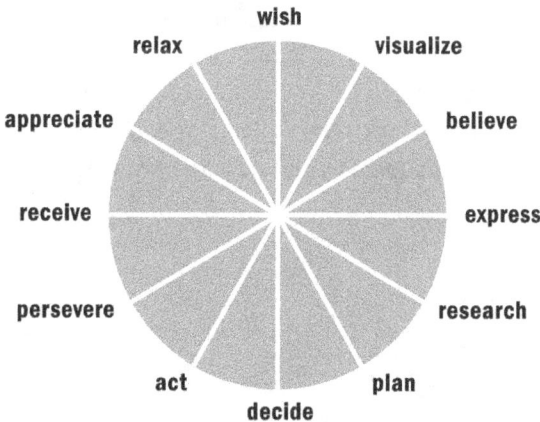

Wish

What do you need in order to realize your wishes? Well, what you need in the first place is a wish! Your own wish, a wish that you have found somewhere inside yourself. A real wish is formulated positively and it will give you a lot of energy. This energy is needed, because there are still eleven steps! Don't worry about how you will realize your wish – this will come later.

Visualize

The next step is to visualize your wish. What does the end result of your wish look like? What do you see in your mind's eye? In this phase you will visualize your wish: in your mind and at a drawing table. It is important to focus on a visible end result; you don't have to visualize the road there (with whom, in what order).

Believe

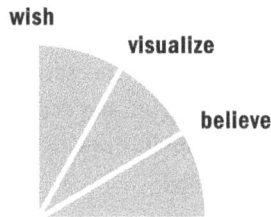

An important step before you can continue is to believe in your dream and in its feasibility. If you don't believe in it, who will? A clear vision from the previous step will help with this. If you do doubt, then consider why this is the case. Do you doubt your wish or do you doubt yourself? If you doubt yourself, you must realize that you won't have to do everything alone. If you have a genuine wish, you will find people in your environment who will help you.

Express

It is now time to express your wish. Express your wish with all your enthusiasm and faith that it will succeed. The more enthusiasm you show, the stronger your message will be. Don't expect everyone to be enthusiastic instantly. You must realize that in whatever way they react, it is a reaction to your wish and not to you as a person. Cherish the people who share your enthusiasm; these people may become your allies in the next step.

Research

The art of living is not to try to do everything yourself. An enterprising person is not someone who can do everything. Someone who does everything alone will become dead tired. The art is to surround yourself with people who can help you. You won't always find them in your own network. Thankfully you believe in your wish (step 3), so you will also be able to find partners away from the trodden path.

Plan

wish

visualize

believe

express

research

plan

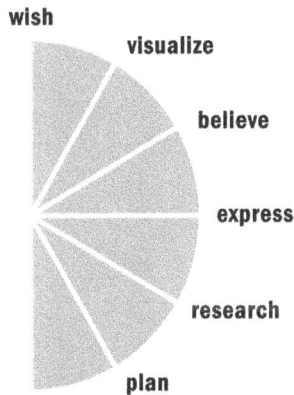

Up till now the whole creation process only took place in the world of words and images. We now need a technique that can bring us from dream to reality. This technique is called planning. Planning takes place exactly on the border between fantasy and reality. That which is planned has a strong tendency to actually come true!

Decide

Based on the plan from the previous step, you and your partners will make a choice: will we do this? Deciding is a difficult step if you skip the visualizing, believing, expressing, research and planning. If you have performed the previous steps with enough attention (including involving the right partners) you will grow towards your decisions and choices.

Act

Now it's time for the real work. You take action; you give all you got. You discover, make use of, and develop your talents together with your partners. Based on your plans you will, step-by-step, turn your wish into a reality.

Persevere

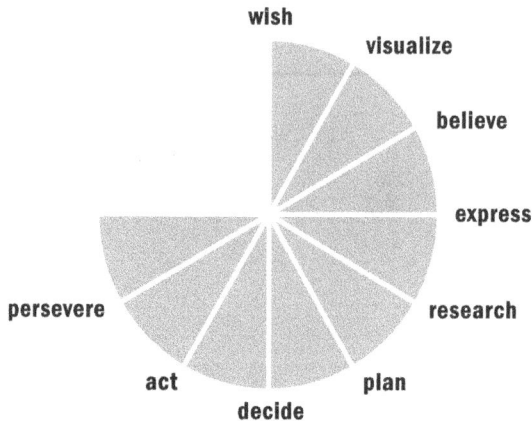

wish
visualize
believe
express
research
plan
decide
act
persevere

You have prepared well, but it turns out that in practice you must overcome unexpected problems. Things take longer than you thought. You're missing certain practical skills. In short: you must persevere. Learn through trial and error. Perseverance is the step in which your faith (step 3) will be tested.

Receive

For many people, receiving is the most difficult step in the whole process of creation. Longing for new success is often easier for us than simply enjoying successes already achieved. Enjoying your achievement will give you energy. You will function better and that is not only pleasant for you, but also for your environment! Receive compliments and pass them on.

Appreciate

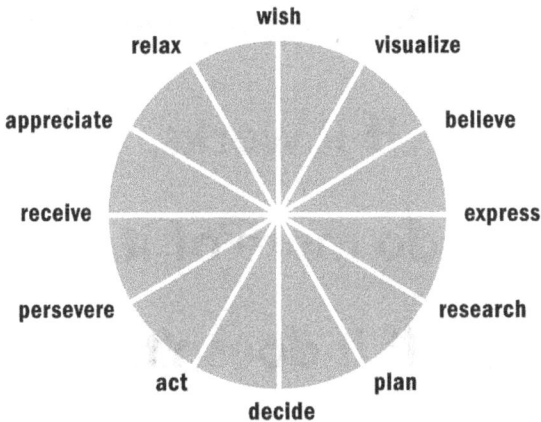

Which people have you met along the way, what have you learned, how have you grown? For this step, you will also look at the matters that were put on hold. What irritated you, what have you been afraid of? Now is the time for a thorough evaluation: have you actually received what you wished for?

Relax

When you have enjoyed your harvest, you can slowly settle down again. A time of reflection. Quietly go to the woods; sit by the fireplace, in a meditation room or a temple. And then you'll come across new wishes. If you spend enough time with yourself, reach and explore the darkness inside of you, new desires will surface and you will discover what you truly wish for in life. The whole process of creation will start afresh. The cycle is complete.

'Do something.

If it works,

do more of it.

If it doesn't,

do something else.'

– Franklin D. Roosevelt –

Who is Esther Jacobs?

Esther Jacobs (1970) has never worked in a regular job: she's been self-employed since the age of 22. She became known as the 'No Excuses Lady' for her charity work. She initiated Coins for Care, a fundraising campaign that collected millions of dollars in foreign currency for charity, surrounding the introduction of the euro. Next, she set up the first Donor Organization in the Netherlands, to promote transparency of charities. In 2005, Esther was a much-discussed participant in the reality show *Survivor*.

© Jeroen van Amelsvoort

Esther has traveled through over one hundred countries and now lives mostly in Curaçao, Miami, Mallorca and Amsterdam. This lover-of-life has designed her life in such a way that she only has to work a few months per year and she's not bound to a single location.

Esther gives motivational speeches and workshops on thinking differently and she writes books and columns. Her motto is, 'if you do what you always did, you will get what you always got', with which she stimulates creative thinking. She coaches entrepreneurs and other people who want to realize their dreams.

Also see: www.estherjacobs.info, subscribe to her '5 minutes of inspiration newsletter' or follow @estherjacobs on Twitter.

© Punkmedia

What is Your Excuse?

Esther Jacobs (1970) has no job, relationship, money, retirement fund, rich family or other securities. Yet she has traveled through more than one hundred countries, she has collected millions of dollars for charity, lives on a tropical island and works but a few months per year.

During her charity campaign Coins for Care she collected leftover foreign coins for charity surrounding the introduction of the euro. Next, she turned the conservative charity world on its head with her call for more transparency. Last but not least she was bullied away from an uninhabited island during the reality show *Survivor*.

Despite all setbacks and hindrances, Esther has continued to smile. She always knew how to turn a situation to her advantage and reach her goals.

How does she do it? Can we learn from it?

Based on her experiences and the most frequently used excuses, Esther takes us along the peaks and valleys that we all encounter in our lives. She shows us that there is never an excuse when you really, wholeheartedly want something.

'Esther dares to move mountains and she actually does it. If need be with her bare hands.' – Kluun

'Our heroine; they were so unreasonable to her on that Survivor island, she didn't stand a chance. She just continued to be human and friendly. How does she do it?' – Linda de Mol

'Esther Jacobs has created quite a stir in the charity world. I admire her for her fight for transparency and the results that she has achieved.' – Morris Tabaksblat

'Esther succeeded at getting a lot of publicity with limited means; this says a lot about her resourcefulness and effort. I recognize in myself her tendency to choose the hard way, because of her strong sense of justice.' – Peter R. de Vries

'This period in time needs people who dare to step away from the ordinary, move boundaries and give rise to new chances. Esther Jacobs is one of those people.' – Herman Wijffels

What has been said about *What is Your Excuse?*

'A book that reads like an adventure story, in which the reader is stimulated not to walk the beaten path.' - Santé

'The book is inspiring, which you should expect from a "make your dreams come true" book, but it has also been written compellingly.' – Susan Smit in *Happinez* Magazine

'I have quit my job and I am going to start my own business.' – reader Bert

'I now realize that things won't happen automatically and I will have to persevere,' – reader Iris

'At Christmas you often get presents of which you think, what on earth do I do with it? Same story this time: a book. However, I read it in one go. Thanks for the wise lessons.' – reader Ruud

'Esther has shown me that problems don't exist; only challenges do.' – reader Danielle

'The book moved me to tears from recognition.' – reader Angelique

'I have gone on unpaid leave in order to travel around the world – ready for adventure!' – reader Saskia

Have you found your Mr. Wong yet?

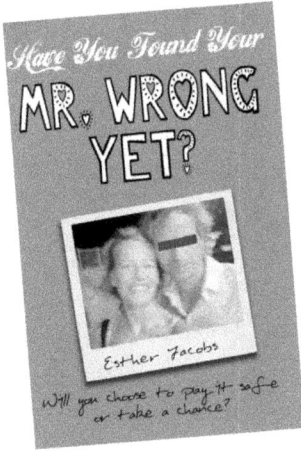

I never thought I would fall for the typical 'Mr. Wrong' of the island. As an intelligent, independent and modern woman a (former) playboy was not exactly what I had in mind for myself. Still, we kept running into each other and there was a definite attraction...

Would he break my heart with his charming ways, his sweet talk and promises that so many women before me had fallen for? Or did he mean it, and was it for real, this time around?

How seriously should I consider the warnings of my friends? Should I listen to my heart or my mind? Should I choose security or adventure?

Can a person really change? And should we strive for that? What does an ambivalent situation like this teach you about your own character, desires and fears?

Slowly I started to realize that the trip was more important than the destination. That I could learn a lot from this situation. That I better try to enjoy the highs, live in the moment and not fear the possible lows. I had to learn to let go. REALLY let go...

Motivational speaker Esther Jacobs decided to research the Mr. Wrong phenomenon. Using her own love story and experience as a starting point, she embarks on a journey exploring our ideas about love, relationships and the truth. Candid interviews with various players and the women who fall for them, explorations of alternative relationship forms, statistics about 'boring bookkeepers who can't be trusted' and also Mrs. Wrongs are all included. Jacobs challenges readers to make their own choices: 'security' or adventure?

'Have you found your Mr. Wong yet?' gives us an unreserved glimpse behind the scenes of a woman who is known for taking unbeaten paths. Who now finds herself repeatedly confronted with all of life's important questions when she falls in love with a... 'special' guy.

I hope you enjoyed reading my book and wish you lots of success and fun with realizing your dreams.

Esther

Spelling errors, typo's or translation hiccups???

I'd love to hear from you! Please help to improve this book by emailing me any suggestions you have on info@estherjacobs.info

www.ingramcontent.com/pod-product-compliance
Lightning Source LLC
Chambersburg PA
CBHW072119270326
41931CB00010B/1607